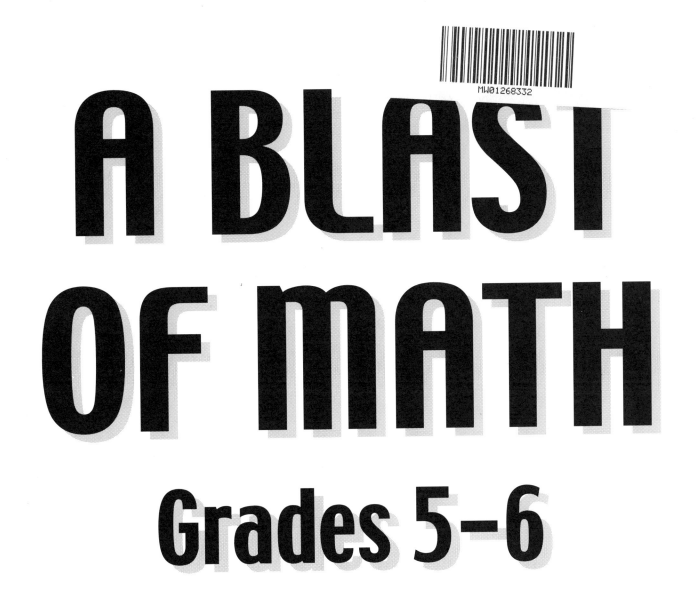

A BLAST OF MATH

Grades 5-6

Written by Gunter Schymkiw
Published by World Teachers Press®

Published with the permission of R.I.C. Publications Pty. Ltd.

First published by R.I.C. Publications Pty. Ltd., Perth, Western Australia. Revised by Didax Educational Resources.

Printed in the United States of America.

Order Number 2-5192
ISBN 1-58324-127-2

A B C D E F 03 02 01

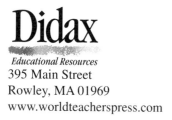

Educational Resources
395 Main Street
Rowley, MA 01969
www.worldteacherspress.com

Foreword

The overall aim of the *A Blast of Math* series is to promote and develop mathematical discussion and student understanding of mathematical concepts within the classroom.

The *A Blast of Math* series features:

- precise mathematical explanations at both students' and teacher's levels
- a structured questioning layout to develop concepts sequentially and lead students to a logical answer
- strong support for the development of listening skills
- simple assessment of student understanding
- ease for the teacher to supply further information as required
- an ideal basis for further mathematical discussion
- an emphasis on student understanding rather than rote "correct" answers
- answers and explanations are provided for quick and easy reference

The concept behind the series could not be easier; students are provided with a worksheet and teachers with an instruction/background sheet. Teachers are supplied with precise instructions to read out to the students, who respond by completing the appropriate section on their worksheet.

The publisher has chosen to use metric measurements for most activities in this book. The National Council of Teachers of Math supports the use of the metric system as an integral part of the mathematics curriculum at all levels of education (NCTM Position Statement on Metrication, 1986). In some activities, Imperial (English) measurements are used for illustrative purposes.

Other titles in the series are: *A Blast of Math* — Grades 3-4
A Blast of Math — Grades 4-5
A Blast of Math — Grades 6-7

Contents

Student progress chart

Name _____

Blast#	Date	Score	Comments/Errors
1		/20	
2		/20	
3		/20	
4		/20	
5		/20	
6		/20	
7		/20	
8		/20	
9		/20	
10		/20	
11		/20	
12		/20	
13		/20	
14		/20	
15		/20	
16		/20	
17		/20	
18		/20	
19		/20	
20		/20	
21		/20	
22		/20	
23		/20	
24		/20	
25		/20	
26		/20	
27		/20	
28		/20	
29		/20	

Teacher's notes

The activities contained in this series are wide and varied and practice a range of general strategies students can use when dealing with mathematical problems across the curriculum. The activities promote a wide range of math concepts in addition to developing listening skills.

Extra information and explanations are included in italics.

Boxed information provides an explanation of the structure of the questioning and guides students to the relevant places on their worksheets.

Answer to each question provided here for easy reference.

Materials needed for the session are listed here.

Answers to extra activities provided, where necessary.

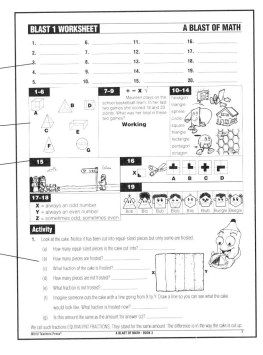

Students answer all questions here.

Information and diagrams needed for questions are supplied on student worksheet.

Each activity is numbered clearly.

Extra activities have been added to consolidate work.

BLAST 1

No.	Question and Discussion	Answer

(i) The first 6 questions are about the pictures that represent solid or 3-D shapes on your sheet. Discuss the three dimensions of length (height), width and depth. Allow children to demonstrate these as follows: length (height) – small jumps up and down; width – step from side to side; depth – step forwards and backwards. Use the letters to write answers.

1. Hector's cheese is a cylinder. Which is Hector's cheese? — D

2. Wolfgang's favorite hat is shaped like a cone. Which is Wolfgang's hat? — F

3. Otto's toy box is a rectangular prism. Which is Otto's toy box? — E

4. Professor Von Schultz has invented hens that lay cube-shaped eggs. Which shape is a Von Schultz egg? — A

5. When a pyramid salesman came to the palace of the Egyptian pharaoh, Ramses, Ramses decided he wanted a square pyramid. Which did he choose? — C

6. One fine morning the people of Toodletown were surprised to find that a sphere-shaped object from a distant galaxy had landed in the park. Which shape is the same as this mysterious spacecraft? — G

(i) Read the problem on your sheet, and then I will ask 3 questions about it. (Read the problem aloud with the class).

7. The first thing we must ask ourselves when doing a problem is, "What am I trying to find out in this problem?" Listen carefully, then answer A, B, or C on the line provided.
A = How many times did Maureen shoot?   B = How many points did she score in the game?
C = The total number of points she scored in the last 2 games. — C

8. Look at the operations symbols above the problem. One of these tells the operation you would use to find the answer to the problem. Which symbol would you use? — +

9. Use the working space to work out the answer. Write your answer on answer line 9. — 41 runs

Discuss the above three steps as a good approach to problem solving. The steps are: WHAT? (What do I have to find out?) HOW? (How can I find the answer; i.e., what operation must I use to find the answer?) Find the answer.

(i) Questions 10 to 14 relate to the pictures of 2-D (or plane) shapes on your sheet. Choose words from the word bank to write your answer.

10. Which shape is Belinda Bee's honey cell? — hexagon

11. Which shape is the front view of the house? — pentagon

12. Which shape is watching the news on television? — square
(Note that a square is a type of rectangle, so the answer "rectangle" can be accepted.)

13. Which shape is jumping rope? — rectangle
(The rectangle shown is an "oblong" – i.e., a rectangle that isn't a square.)

14. Which shape is jogging? — sphere

15. Listen to this very old riddle and see if you can work out the answer. The picture may help you.
As I was going to St. Ives,
I met a man with seven wives:
Each wife had seven cats, Each cat had seven kits;
Kits, cats, sacks and wives,
How many were going to St. Ives? — one
The other people were going the other way.

16. Piece of paper X has been folded into four. The shading shows where a part has been cut out. Which sheet shows what X would look like when unfolded? — C

(i) Choose from X, Y, or Z to answer the next 2 questions.

17. When we multiply an odd number by an odd number our answer is always … (X, Y, or Z). — X

18. What is our answer when we multiply an odd and even number? — Y

19. Listen carefully and try to solve the mystery of who stole the tarts. Try to eliminate at least one suspect with every clue. Circle eliminated suspects as you go. One clue is a "red herring;" that is, it doesn't really have any effect on the solving of the mystery.
Clue 1: He has an odd number of sides. — (Eliminate Bub, Blib, Bugle and Beegle.)
Clue 2: He has curly hair. — (Eliminate Bob.)
Clue 3: His ears are rectangles. — (Eliminate Blob.)
Clue 4: He looks unhappy. — (Red herring clue.)
Clue 5: His nose is a triangle.   Who's the thief? — Blub

20. Within 10 degrees Celsius, estimate the temperature in the room right now. — teacher

Additional Material Needed

Room thermometer

Activity Answers

1. (a) 5   (b) 2   (c) $\frac{2}{5}$ (d) 3   (e) $\frac{3}{5}$ (f) $\frac{4}{10}$ (g) yes

A BLAST OF MATH - BOOK 3

1. _____ 6. _____ 11. _____ 16. _____
2. _____ 7. _____ 12. _____ 17. _____
3. _____ 8. _____ 13. _____ 18. _____
4. _____ 9. _____ 14. _____ 19. _____
5. _____ 10. _____ 15. _____ 20. _____

1–6

A B C D E F G

7–9 + − X ÷

Maureen plays on the school basketball team. In her last two games she scored 18 and 23 points. What was her total in these two games?

Working

10–14

hexagon
triangle
sphere
circle
square
triangle
rectangle
pentagon
octagon

15

St. Ives

16

X ∟ A B C D

17–18

X = always an odd number
Y = always an even number
Z = sometimes odd, sometimes even

19

Bob Bib Bub Blob Blib Blub Bungle Beegle

Activity

1. Look at the cake. Notice it has been cut into equal-sized pieces but only some are frosted.

    (a) How many equal-sized pieces is the cake cut into? _____

    (b) How many pieces are frosted? _____

    (c) What fraction of the cake is frosted? _____

    (d) How many pieces are not frosted? _____

    (e) What fraction is not frosted? _____

    (f) Imagine someone cuts the cake with a line going from X to Y. Draw a line so you can see what the cake would look like. What fraction is frosted now? _____

    (g) Is this amount the same as the amount for answer (c)? _____

We call such fractions EQUIVALENT FRACTIONS. They stand for the same amount. The difference is in the way the cake is cut up.

No.	Question and Discussion	Answer

(i) Read the problem on your sheet, then I will ask you 3 questions about it.

1. The first thing we must ask ourselves when doing a problem is, "What am I trying to find out in this problem?" Listen carefully, then answer A, B, or C.
A = How many words Amy spelled correctly.
B = How many words Amy got wrong.
C = How many words there were in the test.

B

2. Look at the operations symbols above the problem. One of these tells the operation you would use to find the answer to the problem. Which symbol would you use?

−

3. Use the working space to work out the answer. Write your answer on answer line 3.

12 words

(i) Questions 4 to 8 are about the 2-D shapes on your sheet. Their names are written in the word bank along with some 2-D shapes not shown on your sheet.

4. What do we call the eight-sided shape doing a handstand?

octagon

5. There are two shapes with two sets of parallel lines in them. What do we call the one looking for a lost marble in the long grass?

parallelogram

6. The shape mailing a letter has seven sides. Do you know the prefix that means "seven"? If you do, write the name of this shape.

heptagon

7. The shape fainting after seeing a mouse is like a square pushed out of shape. Do you know its name?

rhombus

8. Which shape has just lifted a barbell?

trapezoid

(i) Choose from the possibilities on your sheet to answer the next 4 questions.

9. Is a square a rectangle?

always

10. Is a square an oblong?

never

11. Is an oblong a rectangle?

always

12. Is a rectangle a square?

sometimes

(i) Larry, Sarah, Jim and Bruce are lined up at the gate to go to the show. Write where each child finishes on the grid after following the directions given. Use the letters A to I to answer.

13. Larry goes three right, three up, five right, two down and four left. Where does he finish?

D, the jugglers

14. Sarah goes five right, three up, three left and one up. Where does she finish?

B, the flea circus

15. Jim goes eight right, four up, seven left, four down and one right. Where does he finish?

C, the ghost train

16. Bruce goes one right, four up, four right, two down, three right and two down. Where does he finish?

I, the toad races

17. Look at the towels hung out after the beach. Listen to the clues and you should be able to work out which towel belongs to Jazmin. Eliminate those that don't fit the clues as you go by circling them.
Clue 1: It has an odd number of pictures on it.
Clue 2: At least one of the pictures is a circle.
Clue 3: There are no triangles on her towel.
Clue 4: There are fewer than six pictures on the towel.
Clue 5: The pictures on the towels are not all of the same shape.
Clue 6: Two of the pictures are of living things. Which is Jazmin's towel?

B

18. A fruit juice container holds 250 milliliters of juice. Write this amount using the abbreviation for milliliters on answer line 18.

250 mL

19. What shape has six sides?

hexagon

20. Choose a child from the class. Ask the children to estimate the child's height.

teacher

Additional Material Needed

Something to measure child's height

Activity Answers

1. (a) 45   (b) 70   (c) 260   (d) 35

1. _____	6. _____	11. _____	16. _____
2. _____	7. _____	12. _____	17. _____
3. _____	8. _____	13. _____	18. _____
4. _____	9. _____	14. _____	19. _____
5. _____	10. _____	15. _____	20. _____

1–3   **+ – x ÷**   **Working**

Amy spelled 88 out of the 100 words in spelling test correctly. How many did she get wrong?

4–8

rhombus

octagon

hexagon

heptagon

trapezoid

triangle

parallelogram

9–12

sometimes	never	always

13–16

A = Spider Boy   **B** = Flea Circus   **C** = Ghost Train
D = Jugglers   **E** = Clowns   **F** = Knock 'em Downs
G = Mirror Maze   **H** = Ferris Wheel   **I** = Toad Races

Jim

Bruce

Larry   Sarah

START HERE ➤

17

A   B   C

D   E   F   G

Activity

1. The picture graph shows specimens observed at the beach. Each picture stands for 10 creatures.

(a) How many starfish were seen? _____

(b) How many periwinkles were seen? _____

(c) How many specimens were seen altogether? _____

(d) How many more clams were seen than sea anemones? _____

 = starfish   = seasnails   = periwinkles

 = sea anemones   = clams   = crabs

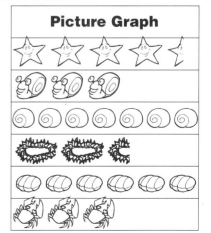

Picture Graph

No.	Question and Discussion	Answer

(i) Read the problem on your sheet, then I will ask you 3 questions about it.

1. The first thing we must ask ourselves when doing a problem is, "What am I trying to find out in this problem?" Listen carefully, then answer A, B, or C.

A = How many sausages have to be ordered?   A
B = How many children at the camp?
C = How many sausages does each child eat?

2. Look at the operations symbols above the problem. One of these tells the operation you would use to find the answer to the problem. Which symbol would you use?   x

3. Use the working space to work out the answer. Write your answer on answer line 3.   96 sausages

4. A kilogram of sausages was left on a bench. The boy who found them and handed them in at the police station gave this description of the owner. The police then went to the bus stop where the seven ladies on your sheet were waiting for the next bus. See if you can find the owner by listening to the clues and circling the ladies that don't belong.
Clue 1: She had glasses.
Clue 2: She had dark shoes.
Clue 3: She had a smile on her face at all times.
Clue 4: She had curly hair.
Clue 5: She had an odd number of dots on her dress.
Clue 6: She didn't have freckles.   Mabel

(i) The next 3 questions are about the areas of the objects in the word bank. Match the areas with the objects as I name them.

5. Which area is closest to that of a postage stamp? 4 cm^2

6. Which area is closest to that of a $10 bill? 120 cm^2

7. Which area is closest to that of a piece of photocopy paper? 660 cm^2

(i) The next 4 questions are about the capacities of the containers listed on the sheet. Match the capacity and container as I name it.

8. Which capacity is closest to that of a can of soft drink?   375 mL

9. Which capacity is closest to that of a bucket?   10 L

10. Which capacity is closest to that of a teacup?   200 mL

11. Which capacity is closest to that of a milk carton?   1 L

(i) The last 9 questions are about the 3-D shapes drawn on your sheet. As we go through them, see if you can discover the pattern for finding the number of faces of a prism.

12. Which shape is a pentagonal prism?   C

13. How many sides does a pentagon have?   5

14. How many faces does a pentagonal prism have?   7

15. Which shape is a triangular prism?   E

16. How many sides does a triangle have?   3

17. How many faces does a triangular prism have?   5

18. Which shape is a hexagonal prism?   D

19. How many sides does a hexagon have?   6

20. How many faces does a hexagonal prism have?   8

Note the link between the number of faces a prism has and the number of sides of its naming face. Ask the class if they can make up a formula for the number of faces of a prism; for example, faces of a prism = number of sides of naming face + 2.

Activity Answers

A nervous wreck

1. _____
6. _____
11. _____
16. _____

2. _____
7. _____
12. _____
17. _____

3. _____
8. _____
13. _____
18. _____

4. _____
9. _____
14. _____
19. _____

5. _____
10. _____
15. _____
20. _____

1–3 — Working

+ − x ÷

There are 32 children at summer camp. Each child has three sausages for breakfast. How many must be ordered to cater for this?

4

Ena Shirley Edna Mabel
Mary Eunice Lydia

5–7

postage stamp

$10 bill

piece of photocopy paper

4 cm²

¹/₂ cm²

1 m²

660 cm²

120 cm²

8–11

1 L

375 mL

200 mL

10 L

can of soft drink

bucket

milk carton

teacup

12–20

A B C D E

Activity

Numeration

What is the place value of 5 in the numerals in the table? Color the letter in the correct column, then write it on the line at the end. When you have finished, use the letters to write the answer to this riddle.

What lies at the bottom of the ocean and shakes?

Answer:

_____

_____ _____ _____ _____ _____ _____ _____

_____ _____ _____ _____

Number	Values					
	50,000	5,000	500	50	5	
44,215	E	G	F	O	A	
63,524	B	F	N	D	E	
57,263	E	G	J	H	I	
45,237	K	R	L	M	C	
41,256	P	R	T	V	U	
36,514	S	Q	O	V	X	
30,105	A	X	Z	W	U	
15,879	F	S	B	D	E	
58,243	W	C	G	H	J	
25,896	K	R	O	M	G	
24,501	Z	L	E	P	R	
96,452	G	M	E	C	S	
85,112	A	K	N	G	O	

BLAST 4

No.	Question and Discussion	Answer

Brenda's mother was born in one of the years shown on your sheet.

1. Listen to the clues to find out the year in which she was born. Cross off years that don't belong as you hear the clues.
Clue 1: It was in the 1960s.
Clue 2: It was an even numbered year.
Clue 3: 1964 and 1968 were Olympic years. There was no Olympic Games in the year we are looking for.
Clue 4: Of the years left, it was the one closest to the 1970s. — 1966

(*i*) The next 15 questions are about the pictures representing pyramids on your sheet. See if you can see a pattern as we do them.

2. Which picture shows a square pyramid? — A
3. How many sides does a square have? — 4
4. How many faces does a square pyramid have? — 5
5. Which picture shows an octagonal pyramid? — E
6. How many sides does an octagon have? — 8
7. How many faces does an octagonal pyramid have? — 9
8. Which picture shows a hexagonal pyramid? — D
9. How many sides does a hexagon have? — 6
10. How many faces does a hexagonal pyramid have? — 7
11. Which picture shows a pentagonal pyramid? — C
12. How many sides does a pentagon have? — 5
13. How many faces does a pentagonal pyramid have? — 6
14. Which picture shows a triangular pyramid? — B
15. How many sides does a triangle have? — 3
16. How many faces does a triangular pyramid have? — 4

Ask the children if they can come up with a formula for finding the number of faces of a pyramid; i.e., number of faces of a pyramid = number of sides of naming face (the base) + 1.

17. How many blocks have been used to make the prism on your sheet? — 16

Allow the children to experiment making cubes and rectangular prisms with centicubes. Some may discover the relationship between the number of cubes and their length, width and height; i.e., volume = length x width x height.

18. If each square on the shaded picture is 1 cm², what is the area of the shape? — $8\frac{1}{2}$ cm²

Remind the children that the diagonal cuts the 3 cm² rectangle into 2 equal-sized triangles of $1\frac{1}{2}$ cm². This is easily demonstrated by cutting a rectangular sheet diagonally and showing how each piece fits exactly over the other.

19. Follow the steps to write 758 centimeters as a length in meters using "decimal notation."
Step 1: Write the total number of meters in 758 centimeters, if any. — 7
Remember that 100 cm makes a meter.
Step 2: Write the decimal point next to separate whole meters from centimeters. — 7.
Step 3: Write the number of centimeters left over. — 7.58
Step 4: Write "m" for meters at the end. — 7.58 m

20. Ask the children to estimate the distance from one point to another in the classroom. According to the distance, allow a reasonable leeway for answers. — teacher

Additional Material Needed

Centicubes, rectangular sheet of paper cut diagonally in half

Activity Answers

1. (a) 5, 4   (b) 1, 3   (c) x   (d) no   (e) 4, 2   (f)

1. _____	6. _____	11. _____	16. _____
2. _____	7. _____	12. _____	17. _____
3. _____	8. _____	13. _____	18. _____
4. _____	9. _____	14. _____	19. _____
5. _____	10. _____	15. _____	20. _____

1

1960	1961	1962	1963	1964	1965	1966	1967
1968	1969	1970	1971	1972	1973	1974	1975

2–16

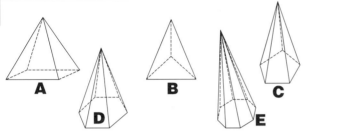

A   B   C

D   E

Formula: _____

17

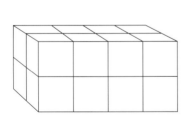

18

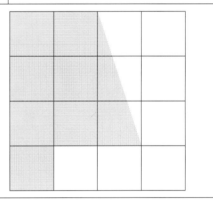

Activity

1. Remember that the horizontal (across) reference in a grid is always written before the vertical (up and down). The sad face is in position 4, 3, not 3, 4. Write the grid location of these:

   (a) What is the sun's position? _____

   (b) What is the position of the smiling face? _____

   (c) Draw the object in 3, 1. _____

   (d) Is the cloud in position 4, 2? _____

   (e) What is the tree's position? _____

   (f) Draw the object in position 3, 3. _____

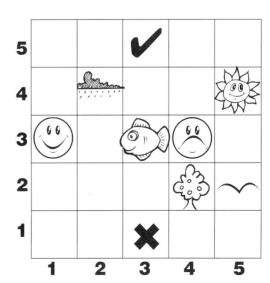

BLAST 5

No.	Question and Discussion	Answer
(i)	Questions 1 to 7 relate to the picture of a cake on your sheet. Notice that it has been cut into four equal-sized pieces and one piece has frosting on it.	
1.	What fraction of the cake has frosting on it?	$^1/_4$
2.	What fraction is not frosted?	$^3/_4$
3.	Dad came in and made the following cuts: A to B, C to D, W to X and Y to Z. Draw lines on these cuts so that you can see what the cake looked like. What fraction (how many out of how many) are frosted now?	$^4/_{16}$
4.	What fraction is not frosted now?	$^{12}/_{16}$
5.	Is $^4/_{16}$ more than $^1/_4$?	no
6.	Is $^4/_{16}$ less than $^1/_4$?	no — the same amount
	It is the same amount, cut up differently. We call $^1/_4$ and $^4/_{16}$ equivalent fractions.	
7.	Are $^3/_4$ and $^{12}/_{16}$ equivalent fractions?	yes
8.	Dan is sending some glasses to his grandmother in the package shown. They are easily broken, so he decides to put a fragile sticker on every face. How many stickers will he need?	6
9.–10.	X and Y are symmetrical shapes. Add their missing halves, then write the letter or number formed on answer lines 9 and 10.	8 and H
11.	How many blocks have been used to make the prism on your sheet?	24
	Allow children to experiment making cubes and rectangular prisms with centicubes. Some may discover the relationship between the number of cubes and the length, width and height; i.e., volume = length x width x height.	
12.	Henry is given three rubber ducks for his birthday. He goes to the bathtub to play with them at 6:45 p.m. and finishes at 9:15 p.m. For how long is he in the bathtub?	2 hrs 30 min
(i)	Choose from the times on your sheet to answer the following questions.	
13.	Write half past 9 using digital notation.	9:30
14.	Write 25 minutes to 12 using digital notation.	11:35
15.	Write 2 minutes past 3 using digital notation.	3:02
16.	Use any of the operations symbols to make the three threes on your sheet equal 3.	teacher
17.	Use any of the operations symbols to make the five fives equal 5.	teacher
(i)	The last 3 questions are about Kerry, Terry and Jerry. They live in Windy City and attend Squall School. Choose from the words in the word bank to describe the ways their ties hang.	
18.	Kerry uses an industrial-strength tie clip to clip his tie to his shirt. Which word describes the way it hangs?	vertical
19.	Terry has concealed an iron bar inside his tie so that it remains straight. Unfortunately the wind is so strong that the tie still makes this sort of line.	oblique
20.	Jerry's tie is made of crepe paper. A few seconds after this picture was taken the principal of the school, Mr. Thunder, said, "Straighten your tie son! It's …"?	horizontal

Additional Material Needed

Centicubes

Activity Answers

When it's raining cats and dogs.

BLAST 5 WORKSHEET

A BLAST OF MATH

1. _____   6. _____   11. _____   16. _____

2. _____   7. _____   12. _____   17. _____

3. _____   8. _____   13. _____   18. _____

4. _____   9. X = _____   14. _____   19. _____

5. _____   10. Y = _____   15. _____   20. _____

1–7	8	9–10	11
A C W X Y Z B D		X = Y =	

13–15			
3:2	3:20	3:02	9$\frac{1}{2}$
9:30	9:12	11:25	11:35
12:25	25:12	11:12	12:05

16–17
+   −   X   ÷
3 ___ 3 ___ 3 = 3
5 ___ 5 ___ 5 ___ 5 ___ 5 = 5

18–20 horizontal | vertical | oblique

Kerry   Terry   Jerry

Activity

Measurement

Match the measurement to what it measures. Color the letter in the correct column, then write it on the line at the end. When you have finished, use the letters to write the answer to this riddle:

What is the worst weather for rats and mice?

___ ___ ___ ___ ___

___ ___ ___ , ___

___ ___ ___ ___ ___ ___

___ ___ ___ ___ ___ ___ .

Measurement	Measures					
	Capacity	Length	Mass	Temperature	Time	
375 mL	W	A	B	M	L	
10 cm	B	H	C	J	K	
500 g	A	C	E	I	H	
4 degrees Celsius	E	F	D	N	G	
60 min	D	C	E	B	I	
freezing point	B	F	A	T	S	
1 km	G	S	Z	G	H	
1 kg	C	H	R	Y	D	
70 L	A	I	X	F	E	
50 min	V	W	J	K	I	
20 tons	U	R	N	L	M	
boiling point	L	O	J	I	N	
5 yrs	D	M	I	O	N	
15 kg	P	H	G	Q	R	
30 sec	T	H	S	O	C	
20 g	G	P	A	F	D	
100 mL	T	Q	B	C	E	
100 km	R	S	U	V	X	
24 hrs	Z	W	S	T	A	
57°C	A	V	T	N	Z	
100 tons	R	U	D	R	S	
1 kL	D	L	V	O	Q	
30 m	G	O	F	W	P	
−4°C	H	I	N	G	X	
1 wk	M	J	E	Y	S	

BLAST 6

No.	Question and Discussion	Answer
(i)	The first 10 questions are about the pictures representing prisms on your sheet. See if you can find the pattern that lets us make a rule (or formula) as we do these.	
1.	Which picture represents an octagonal prism?	B
2.	An octagon has eight sides. How many edges does an octagonal prism have?	24
3.	Which picture represents a pentagonal prism?	C
4.	A pentagon has five sides. How many edges does a pentagonal prism have?	15
5.	Which picture represents a square prism?	A
6.	A square has four sides. How many edges does a square prism have?	12
7.	Which picture represents a hexagonal prism?	E
8.	A hexagon has six sides. How many edges does a hexagonal prism have?	18
9.	Which picture represents a triangular prism?	F
10.	A triangle has three sides. How many edges does a triangular prism have?	9
11.	If each square on the shaded shape has an area of one square centimeter, what is the area of the shape?	14 cm^2

The triangle takes up half of a 12 cm^2 rectangle and so covers 6 cm^2.
There are 8 more squares to be added to this amount, making an area of 14 cm^2 altogether.

No.	Question and Discussion	Answer
12.	Use the code to make the word meaning "a period of one thousand years." Write the word on answer line 12.	millennium
(i)	The next 3 questions are about the cake drawn on your sheet. Al wants to eat the frosted slices.	
13.	What fraction does he want to eat?	$^2/_5$
14.	Before he does this, Belinda comes along. She is hungry but doesn't like to eat big slices. She suggests that the cake be cut from point M to N. Do this by drawing a line from M to N with your pencil. Then she says she would like to eat three of the smaller slices without frosting on them. What fraction will she eat?	$^3/_{10}$
15.	What fraction of the cake has been eaten altogether?	$^7/_{10}$

Demonstrate the more conventional setting out of this type of problem:
$^2/_5 + ^3/_{10} = ^4/_{10} + ^3/_{10} = ^7/_{10}$

No.	Question and Discussion	Answer
16.	I am thinking of a number. Listen to the clues and work out the answer. Clue 1: It is a single digit number. Clue 2: It is more than half a dozen. Clue 3: It is an odd number. Clue 4: You can't divide it evenly by three. It is …	7
(i)	The next 3 questions are about the saucepans on the stove hotplates. Look at the temperatures, then use the letters to answer the questions.	
17.	Which has been filled with water from the hot water faucet in the kitchen and put on the stove about five seconds ago?	A
18.	Which has been filled with water from the cold water faucet and put on the stove about five seconds ago?	C
19.	Which is boiling?	B
20.	Look at the measuring cup. Notice that I have water in it that goes up to …milliliters on the scale. I am going to drop this object into the cup and the water should move up the scale the same number of milliliters as the volume of the object in centicubes (or cubic centimeters). A milliliter of water takes up the same amount of space as a centicube (we call this amount of space a "cubic centimeter"). How many cubic centimeters of volume do you think the object takes up?	teacher

Additional Material Needed

Beaker partly-filled with water, scaled in milliliters; simple object for displacement, e.g., a stone

Activity Answers

1. (a) 3, 4 (b) 2, 3 (c) 4, 1 (d) 6, 5 (e) 6, 1

1. _____   6. _____   11. _____   16. _____
2. _____   7. _____   12. _____   17. _____
3. _____   8. _____   13. _____   18. _____
4. _____   9. _____   14. _____   19. _____
5. _____   10. _____   15. _____   20. _____

1–10

A B C D E F

11

12

CODE			
A=1	H=8	O=15	V=22
B=2	I=9	P=16	W=23
C=3	J=10	Q=17	X=24
D=4	K=11	R=18	Y=25
E=5	L=12	S=19	Z=26
F=6	M=13	T=20	
G=7	N=14	U=21	

A ___ ___ ___ ___ ___ ___ ___ ___ ___
   6+7 3x3 3x4 4x3 10-5 7x2 2x7 4+5 7x3 6+7

is a period of 1,000 years.

13–15

M●   ●N

16

1 2 3 4 5 6 7 8 9 10 11 12

17–19

50°C   100°C   20°C
 A   B   C

Activity

1. Answer the following questions. Remember to write horizontal grid coordinates before the vertical ones and put a comma between them. The crab is at position 5, 2. The bug is at position 2, 5.

   (a) What are the grid coordinates of the little girl? _____

   (b) Where is the dog that has taken her ball? _____

   (c) You can't see the dog catcher but you can see his net. What is its position? _____

   (d) The duck is astonished by what is going on and is keeping a safe distance. What are her coordinates? _____

   (e) The grub moves 2 down and 1 right to be safe. What is its new position? _____

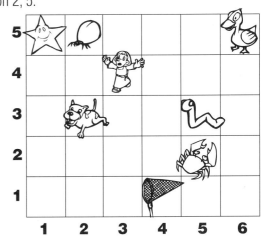

No.	Question and Discussion	Answer
1.	How many blocks have been used to make the prism on your sheet?	40
2.	Is a ton of bricks heavier than, the same as, or lighter than a ton of pillows?	same

ⓘ The next 3 questions are about the picture of a cake on your sheet.

No.	Question and Discussion	Answer
3.	Tiffany wants to eat the frosted pieces. What fraction does she want to eat?	$^3/_5$
4.	Before she eats this, Joshua comes along. He cuts the cake into smaller, equal-sized pieces by cutting from points A to B. Draw a line here so you can see what the cake looks like. He eats three of the smaller pieces without frosting. What fraction of the cake does he eat?	$^3/_{10}$
5.	What fraction of the cake was eaten altogether?	$^9/_{10}$

Demonstrate $^3/_5 + ^3/_{10} = ^6/_{10} + ^3/_{10} = ^9/_{10}$

No.	Question and Discussion	Answer
6.	Audrey is visiting her friend Bridget's house for the first time. Can you help her find it? Listen to the descriptions and cross off houses that it couldn't be as you go. Clue 1: It has a chimney. Clue 2: The chimney is on the left-hand side as you look at the house. Clue 3: It has an even number of windows. Clue 4: The television antenna is on the left-hand side as you look at the house.	C

ⓘ Questions 7 to 10 are about the shapes on the grid. On your answer line, draw the shapes.

No.	Question and Discussion	Answer
7.	Draw the shape at 3, 5.	triangle
8.	Draw the shape at 2, 6.	hexagon
9.	Draw the shape at 2, 3.	circle
10.	What is the position of the fish? Your answer should contain two numbers separated by a comma.	4, 2
11.	If each square on the shaded shape has an area of one square centimeter, what is the shape's area?	8 cm^2
12.	I'm thinking of a capital letter. It is made up of one vertical and two oblique lines. What is it?	K or Y

ⓘ To answer the next 3 questions, you will have to write the names of different seasons. Look at the word bank if you are uncertain of spelling.

No.	Question and Discussion	Answer
13.	Which season follows summer?	fall
14.	Which season is it in June, July and August?	summer
15.	Which season spans the end of one year and the beginning of the next?	winter
16.	If one mouse + one mouse = two mice and one louse + one louse = two lice, what does one house + one house equal?	two houses

ⓘ Containers A, B, C, D and E each hold 1,000 milliliters, or one liter. Match each picture with the likely capacity of liquid it is holding.

No.	Question and Discussion	Answer
17.	Which matches A?	100 mL
18.	Which matches C?	500 mL
19.	Which matches D?	750 mL
20.	Which matches E?	250 mL

Activity Answers

1.   (a) 22   (b) 28   (c) 27   (d) 44   (e) 6W   (f) 16

A BLAST OF MATH

1. _____   6. _____   11. _____   16. _____

2. _____   7. _____   12. _____   17. _____

3. _____   8. _____   13. _____   18. _____

4. _____   9. _____   14. _____   19. _____

5. _____   10. _____   15. _____   20. _____

1

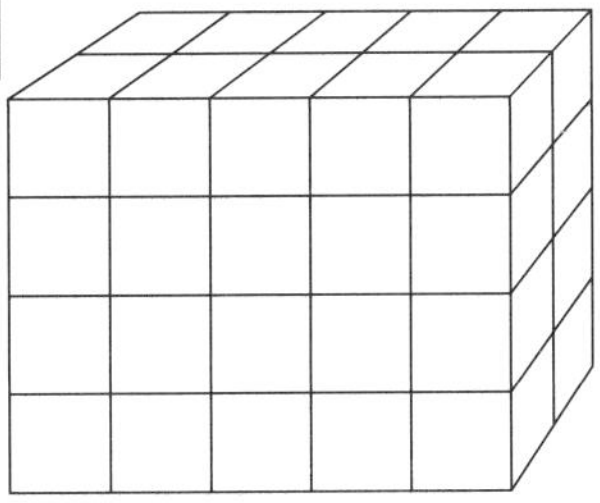

2

| heavier | lighter | same |

3–5

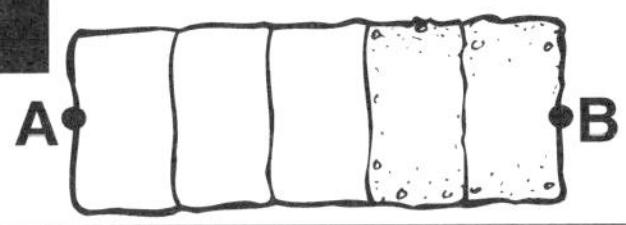

A •   • B

6

A   B   C   D   E   F

7–10

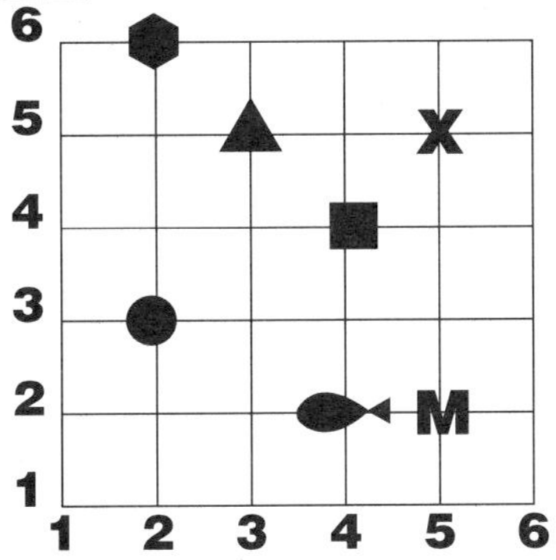

11

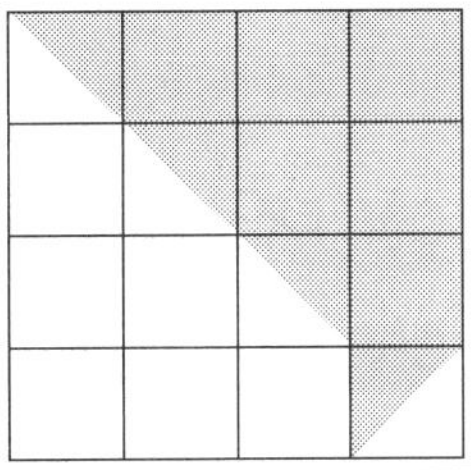

12

A B C D E F G H I
J K L M N O P Q W
R S T U V W X Y Z

13–15

| spring | summer |
| fall | winter |

16

1 mouse + 1 mouse = 2 mice
1 louse + 1 louse = 2 lice
1 house + 1 house = ?

17–20

| 100 mL |
| 500 mL |
| 250 mL |
| 1 L |
| 750 mL |

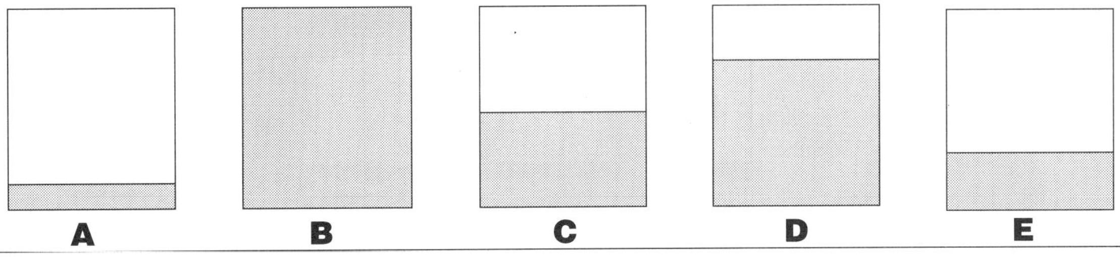

A   B   C   D   E

Activity

1. The graph shows the number of books borrowed by classes from a school library. Each picture of a book stands for 4 books borrowed.

   (a) How many books did Room 3X borrow? _____

   (b) How many books did Room 3Y borrow? _____

   (c) How many books did Room 4B borrow? _____

   (d) How many books did Room 5A and 5F borrow? _____

   (e) Which class borrowed the same number as Room 4B? _____

   (f) How many more books were borrowed by Room 6Q than Room 5A?

Key ☐ = 4 books

3 X
3 Y
4 B
4 Z
5 A
5 F
6 Q
6 W

BLAST 8

No.	Question and Discussion	Answer

1. Listen to the clues to find the name of the English king who told the tide to stop coming in. He did not expect it to stop coming in. He did this to prove to some foolish servants that he did not have powers like a god. Cross off those that don't belong as you hear the clues.

Clue 1: His name has fewer than 7 letters.
Clue 2: The name does not start with a vowel.
Clue 3: The last letter is a vowel.
Clue 4: All the letters in the name are different.   Canute

2. There is only one number that gives a greater result when you add it to itself than when you multiply it by itself. It is one of the five numbers on your answer line. Check them, then circle the correct number. 1

3. Write 25 past 9 in digital time.   9:25

4. At which of the times on your sheet would it normally be warmest?   12 noon

5. Within five centimeters, how long do you think the wiggly line is?   teacher

   Check answers with string.

6. If each square on the shaded shape has an area of one square centimeter, what is the area of the shaded shape?   19 cm^2

ⓘ The next 5 questions are about the picture of a cake on your sheet.

7. Graeme wants to eat the frosted pieces. What fraction of the cake does he want to eat? $^3/_4$
Before he eats them Phyllis comes along. She cuts the cake into smaller, equal-sized pieces by cutting from A to B, C to D, E to F, G to H, I to J, K to L, M to N, and O to P and then from 1 to 2, 3 to 4, 5 to 6, 7 to 8, 9 to 10, 11 to 12, 13 to 14, and 15 to 16. Draw these lines so you can see what the cake looks like.

8. She eats 17 of the smaller pieces without frosting. What fraction of the cake does she eat? $^{17}/_{100}$

9. What fraction of the cake was eaten altogether? $^{92}/_{100}$
   Demonstrate $^3/_4 + {}^{17}/_{100} = {}^{75}/_{100} + {}^{17}/_{100} = {}^{92}/_{100}$

10. Write the fraction that Graeme ate as a decimal.   0.75

11. Write the fraction that Phyllis ate as a decimal.   0.17

ⓘ The next 5 questions are about the temperature map on your sheet. It shows the minimum and maximum temperatures in Australian State and Territory capital cities in one day.

12. What was the maximum temperature in Brisbane on that day?   34°C

13. Which city had the highest maximum on that day?   Darwin

14. Which had the lowest minimum?   Hobart

15. Which city had the largest variation from maximum to minimum?   Melbourne

16. Which season do you think it was?   summer

ⓘ The next 4 questions are about the angles on your sheet. Use the code to work out the names of the angles.

17. XYZ =   acute

18. RST =   obtuse

19. ABC =   right

20. PQR =   straight

Additional Material Needed

String to check answer 5

Activity Answers

1. (a) C, 3, 6 (b) A, 4, 8 (c) D, 5, 10 (d) E, 6, 12 (e) B, 8, 16

2. Number of sides of the base shape x 2.

1. _____   6. _____   11. _____   16. _____

2. 1 2 3 4 5   7. _____   12. _____   17. _____

3. _____   8. _____   13. _____   18. _____

4. _____   9. _____   14. _____   19. _____

5. _____   10. _____   15. _____   20. _____

1	Canute	Alfred	Edward	**4**			
Louis	George	Charles	Arthur	7:00 a.m.	12 noon	7:00 p.m.	

6

7–11

```
    A C E G    I K M O
1 •┌─────────┬─────────┐• 2
3 •│         │         │• 4
5 •│         │         │• 6
7 •│         │         │• 8
   ├─────────┼─────────┤
9 •│         │         │• 10
11•│         │         │• 12
13•│         │         │• 14
15•└─────────┴─────────┘• 16
    B D F H    J L N P
```

5

12–16

D 30 – 37°C
NT
Qld
B 20 – 34°C
WA
SA
S 18 – 31°C
P 20 – 36°C
NSW
A 26 – 32°C
Vic
M 12 – 30°C
Tas
H 11 – 23°C

CODE

A = 4	H = 20	O = 36 V = 70
B = 7	I = 25	P = 37 W = 75
C = 9	J = 26	Q = 38 X = 80
D = 11	K = 27	R = 42 Y = 90
E = 16	L = 28	S = 48 Z = 100
F = 17	M = 29	T = 64
G = 18	N = 30	U = 66

D = Darwin B = Brisbane
S = Sydney P = Perth
H = Hobart A = Adelaide
M = Melbourne

17–20

XYZ= ____ ____ ____ ____ ____
2 x 2   3 x 3   2 x 33   60 + 4   2 x 8

ABC= ____ ____ ____ ____ ____
7 x 6   5 x 5   9 x 2   4 x 5   100 – 36

RST= ____ ____ ____ ____ ____
6 x 6   4 + 3   2 x 32   6 x 11   4 x 12   2 x 8

PQR= ____ ____ ____ ____ ____
6 x 8   84 – 20   6 x 7   9 – 5   30 – 5   3 x 6   5 x 4   34 + 30

Activity

1.

Which is a :	How many sides has a:	How many edges has a:
(a) triangular pyramid? _____	triangle? _____	triangular pyramid? _____
(b) square pyramid? _____	square? _____	square pyramid? _____
(c) pentagonal pyramid? _____	pentagon? _____	pentagonal pyramid? _____
(d) hexagonal pyramid? _____	hexagon? _____	hexagonal pyramid? _____
(e) octagonal pyramid? _____	octagon? _____	octagonal pyramid? _____

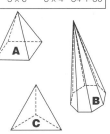

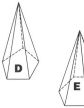

2. Can you work out a formula for the number of edges a pyramid has? _____

BLAST 9

No.	Question and Discussion	Answer
1.	Which of the two fractions in the group are equivalent (i.e., stand for the same amount?)?	$\frac{1}{4}$, $\frac{2}{8}$
2.	Look at today's long date written on the blackboard. Write tomorrow's short date on the answer line.	teacher
3.	Where's Billy? Can you find him? Listen to the clues and cross off the people who aren't Billy. Billy will be the last one left standing unmarked.	
	Clue 1: He is wearing glasses.	
	Clue 2: His pants are white.	
	Clue 3: He's smiling happily.	
	Clue 4: His shoes are black.	
	Clue 5: His hair is straight, not curly.	B

ⓘ Match the times on the analog clock with their digital counterparts.

No.	Question and Discussion	Answer
4.	Which analog clock matches digital clock X?	A
5.	Which digital clock matches analog clock B?	Y
6.	Write the remaining matching pair.	C and Z

ⓘ The next 4 questions are about the map on your sheet. It is drawn to scale so that one centimeter represents two kilometers. Use your ruler to measure the distances, then convert them to kilometers.

No.	Question and Discussion	Answer
7.	How many kilometers is it from Brookbank to Netherville?	2 km
8.	How many kilometers from Riverton to Norville?	12 km
9.	If traveling from Riverton to Faraway, which route is shorter: via Norville or via Centerville?	Norville
10.	The people of Laketown have to catch a ferry to get to Brookbank. How far is the round trip (i.e., there and back)?	16 km

ⓘ The next 2 questions concern the angles on the inside of the noses of Frazzle and Frizzle. Choose from the word bank to give the correct angle name.

No.	Question and Discussion	Answer
11.	What sort of angle does Frazzle's nose form?	acute
12.	What sort of angle does Frizzle's nose form?	obtuse
13.	If each square on the shaded shape has an area of one square centimeter, what is the area of the shape?	18.5 cm^2
14.	If two apples cost $1.00, how much would you pay for one?	50¢
15.	If three bananas cost 60¢, how much would you pay for one?	20¢
16.	If five candies cost 50¢, how much would you pay for one?	10¢
17.	If two yo-yos cost $10.00, how much would you pay for three?	$15.00
18.	Line AD on the diagram on your sheet is a diagonal. Draw another diagonal on the diagram and write its name on the answer line.	BC or CB
19.	Which year in the group on your sheet is in the 18th century?	1797
20.	One container holds 3 L 250 mL. Another holds 1 L 150 mL. How much do they hold altogether? Work it out on your sheet, then write the answer on the answer line.	4 L 400 mL

Additional Material Needed

Today's long date written on the blackboard, each child needs a ruler

Activity Answers

Because 7 8 9 (seven ate nine).

1. _____
2. _____
3. _____
4. _____
5. _____

6. _____
7. _____
8. _____
9. _____
10. _____

11. _____
12. _____
13. _____
14. _____
15. _____

16. _____
17. _____
18. _____
19. _____
20. _____

1

| 1/4 | 1/2 |
| 3/4 | 2/8 |

3

A   B   C   D   E   F   G

4–6

X	Y	Z
9:55	9:35	10:05

A   B   C

7–10

Norville

Centerville

Riverton

Faraway

Netherville

Brookbank

Laketown

11–12

right

acute

obtuse

straight

Frazzle   Frizzle

13

18

A   B

C   D

19

| 1686 | 1797 | 1853 |

20

| 3 L 250 mL |
| 1 L 150 mL |

Activity

Riddle

The answer to this riddle is three consecutive numbers under 10.

Question: Why was 6 afraid of 7?

Answer: Because _____ _____ _____.

BLAST 10

No.	Question and Discussion	Answer
1.	Listen to the clues to work out the number I am talking about. Clue 1: It is a bigger number than the number of weeks in a year. Clue 2: It isn't an even number. Clue 3: It's less than 57. Clue 4: You can't divide it evenly by 5 so it must be …	53
2.	Write twenty-five thousand, six hundred twelve in numerals.	25,612
3.	Now write the numeral for one more than this.	25,613
4.	Now write the numeral for one less than twenty-five thousand, six hundred and twelve.	25,611
5.	What is the volume of the prism on your sheet? Answer in cubic centimeters.	70 cm^3
6.	What fractions in the group on your sheet are equivalent?	$\frac{1}{4}$ and $\frac{2}{8}$
7.	Write "yes" or "no" for the following statement: $4\frac{1}{2}$ kilometers, 4.5 kilometers and 4 kilometers 500 meters are all the same length.	yes
8.	Questions 8 to 13 are about the pentagon on your sheet. AC and AD are diagonals. Is BD a diagonal? If your answer is "yes," write "yes" on the answer line, then draw it.	yes
9.	Is DE a diagonal? Answer "yes" or "no." If your answer is "yes" draw it on the pentagon.	no
10.	Is BE a diagonal? Answer "yes" or "no." If your answer is "yes" draw it on the pentagon.	yes
11.	Is AB a diagonal? Answer "yes" or "no." If your answer is "yes" draw it on the pentagon.	no
12.	Is CE a diagonal? Answer "yes" or "no." If your answer is "yes" draw it on the pentagon.	yes
13.	How many diagonals does a pentagon have?	5
14.	If each square on the diagram has an area of one square centimeter, what is the area of the shaded shape?	14 cm^2
15.	The Normans, people from Normandy in France, successfully invaded England in the year on your sheet that is in the 11th century. In which year was this invasion?	1066
(i)	Questions 16 to 18 relate to the abacus pictures on your sheet.	
16.	What number is shown on Abacus A?	65,123
17.	What is shown on Abacus B?	76,548
18.	Add two more beads to the thousands rail of Abacus C, then write the new number shown.	25,864
19.	One container holds 2 L 500 mL. Another holds 5 L 750 mL. Do the addition, then write the total amount they hold on answer line 19.	8 L 250 mL
20.	Write 8.255 km as kilometers and meters.	8 km 255 m

Activity Answers

1. (a) 8   **2.** (a) 4   **3.** (a) 5   **4.** (a) 6   **5.** (a) 3
  (b) 9   (b) 5   (b) 6   (b) 7   (b) 4

1. _____	6. _____	11. _____	16. _____
2. _____	7. _____	12. _____	17. _____
3. _____	8. _____	13. _____	18. _____
4. _____	9. _____	14. _____	19. _____
5. _____	10. _____	15. _____	20. _____

1 | 50 | 51 | 52 | 53 | 54 | 55 | 56 | 57 | 58 | 59 | 60

2–4 twenty-five thousand six hundred twelve

5

5 cm — 2 cm — 7 cm

6

| 1/4 | 1/2 |
| 3/4 | 2/8 |

7

| 4 1/2 km | 4.5 km |
| 4 kilometers | 500 meters |

8–13

14

15 | 988 | 1066 | 1172 | 1215

16–18

A   B   C

10th th h t u   10th th h t u   10th th h t u

19

2 L 500 mL
+ 5 L 750 mL
_____

Activity

Corners of a Pyramid

1. Picture A shows an octagonal pyramid.
   (a) How many sides does an octagon have? _____
   (b) How many corners does an octagonal pyramid have? _____

2. Picture B shows a square pyramid.
   (a) How many sides does a square have? _____
   (b) How many corners does a square pyramid have? _____

3. Picture C shows a pentagonal pyramid.
   (a) How many sides does a pentagon have? _____
   (b) How many corners does a pentagonal pyramid have? _____

4. Picture D shows a hexagonal pyramid.
   (a) How many sides does a hexagon have? _____
   (b) How many corners does a hexagonal pyramid have? _____

5. Picture E shows a triangular pyramid.
   (a) How many sides does a triangle have? _____
   (b) How many corners does a triangular pyramid have? _____

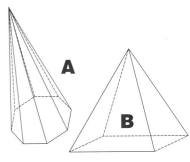

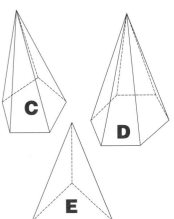

BLAST 11

No.	Question and Discussion	Answer
1.	Which two fractions on your sheet are equivalent?	$^3/_5$ and $^6/_{10}$
2.	Listen to the clues and cross off numbers that don't belong. The number that is left is called a "gross."	
	Clue 1: It is an even number.	
	Clue 2: It doesn't end in zero.	
	Clue 3: Its digits add up to 9. It must be …	144
3.	Write 2.655 kilometers in kilometers and meters on the answer line.	2 km 655 m
4.	How many millimeters in 2 centimeters?	20 mm
5.	Close your eyes and count to estimate the number of seconds between when I say "start" and "stop." Your answer should end in zero or five.	teacher
	Allow the stopwatch to run for 55 seconds.	

(i) Questions 6 to 9 are about the picture of a hexagon on your sheet.

6.	Shape UVWXYZ is a hexagon. UW, UX and UY are diagonals. Draw two new diagonals beginning from W and write their names on your answer line.	WY and WZ
7.	Draw three diagonals from V and write their names on the answer line.	VX, VY and VZ
8.	Draw the remaining diagonal from X and write its name on the answer line.	XZ
9.	How many diagonals are there altogether in a hexagon?	9
10.	Draw cut lines AA, BB etc. on cake A, then write the equivalent fraction you make from $^1/_4$.	$^{25}/_{100}$
11.	Do the same for cake B, and write the equivalent fraction for $^3/_4$.	$^{75}/_{100}$
12.	Christopher Columbus landed in America in the year on your sheet that is in the 15th century. Which year is it?	1492

(i) Questions 13 to 17 are about the picture of a cake on your sheet.

13.	Don wants to eat the frosted pieces. What fraction does he want to eat?	$^3/_{10}$
14.	Before he can do this, Barry comes along. He cuts the cake into smaller equal-sized pieces by cutting from points A to B, C to D, E to F, G to H, I to J, K to L, M to N, O to P and Q to R. Draw the cut lines so you can see what the cake looks like. He eats 35 of the smaller pieces without frosting. What fraction of the cake does he eat?	$^{35}/_{100}$
15.	What fraction of the cake was eaten altogether?	$^{65}/_{100}$
	Demonstrate $^3/_{10} + ^{35}/_{100} = ^{30}/_{100} + ^{35}/_{100} = ^{65}/_{100}$	
16.	Write the fraction that Don ate as a decimal.	0.30 or 0.3
	Just as it is legitimate to write the whole number 3 as 03 or 003, etc., it is also legitimate to write 0.3 as 0.30, 0.300, etc. In general the shorter form is preferred.	
17.	Write the fraction Barry ate as a decimal.	0.35

(i) Listen to the clues, then write the letter that matches the description of the 3-D shape.

18.	I have one round face and one curved surface. Which shape am I?	E
19.	I have five faces and five corners (points, vertices). Which shape am I?	B
20.	I have two round faces and one curved surface. Which shape am I?	C

Additional Material Needed

Stopwatch

Activity Answers

1. 4 **2.** 5, 1 **3.** 1, 2 **4.** swimming pool **5.** 2 km

1. _____	6. _____	11. _____	16. _____
2. _____	7. _____	12. _____	17. _____
3. _____	8. _____	13. _____	18. _____
4. _____	9. _____	14. _____	19. _____
5. _____	10. _____	15. _____	20. _____

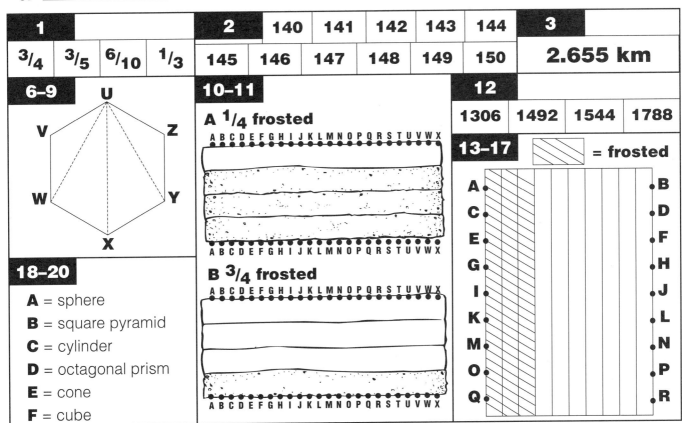

1

| ³/₄ | ³/₅ | ⁶/₁₀ | ¹/₃ |

2

| 140 | 141 | 142 | 143 | 144 |
| 145 | 146 | 147 | 148 | 149 | 150 |

3

2.655 km

6–9

10–11

A **¹/₄ frosted**

A B C D E F G H I J K L M N O P Q R S T U V W X

A B C D E F G H I J K L M N O P Q R S T U V W X

B **³/₄ frosted**

A B C D E F G H I J K L M N O P Q R S T U V W X

A B C D E F G H I J K L M N O P Q R S T U V W X

12

| 1306 | 1492 | 1544 | 1788 |

13–17   = frosted

18–20

A = sphere
B = square pyramid
C = cylinder
D = octagonal prism
E = cone
F = cube

Activity

Street Map

The street map is drawn to scale with 2 cm on the map representing 1 km of actual length. ● = traffic lights.

1. How many sets of traffic lights must you go through if traveling from the post office to the train station? _____

2. What are the coordinates of the intersection of Zap St. and Thunder Road? _____

3. In which grid space is the tennis court? _____

4. Which landmark is located at position 2, 6?

   _____

5. As the crow flies (i.e., in a straight line) how far is it from Duck Swamp to the swimming pool? _____

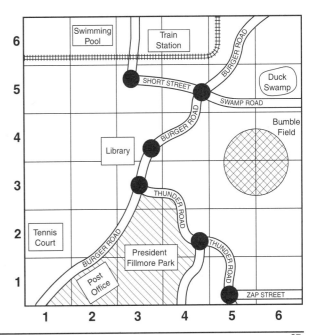

BLAST 12

No.	Question and Discussion	Answer

1. Which of the structures on your sheet would be the most difficult to push out of shape? — triangle

We call shapes that can not be pushed out of shape "rigid." Triangles are rigid shapes. This is important knowledge in building.

2. Which statement (A, B, or C) is correct? — A

Point out where B and C are flawed.

3. One container has a capacity of 4 L 200 mL and another holds 6 L 750 mL. Do the addition, then write the total capacity on answer line 3. — 10 L 950 mL

(i) The next 6 questions are about the octagon on your sheet.

4. AC, AD, AE, AF and AG are diagonals. Draw five new diagonals starting from B and list them on the answer line. — BD, BE, BF, BG, BH

5. Draw four new diagonals from C and list them on answer line 5. — CE, CF, CG, CH

6. Draw three new diagonals from D and list them on answer line 6. — DF, DG, DH

7. Draw two new diagonals from E and list them on answer line 7. — EG, EH

8. Draw the remaining diagonal from F and write its name on the answer line. — FH

9. How many diagonals does an octagon have altogether? Count those that you have listed as well as the five that were already drawn. — 20

10. Ron, Elliott and Wallace Mouse are all hungry. They are very fair mice and decide to share their cheese by each having three equal-sized pieces. Color each mouse's share a different color. What fraction does each mouse eat? — $^3/_{10}$

11. What fraction of the cheese is eaten altogether? — $^9/_{10}$

12. Write the total amount eaten as a decimal. — 0.9

13. Write down the length, width and height of the rectangular prism I am thinking of, then write its volume in cubic centimeters.

Length = 3 cm Width = 4 cm Height = 5 cm — 60 cm³

14. Stacey wants to buy a new dress. Listen to the clues and cross off dresses that don't belong. You will be left with the one she chooses.

Clue 1: She doesn't like polka dots.
Clue 2: She doesn't like vertical stripes.
Clue 3: She likes horizontal stripes even less.
Clue 4: Checks are her least favorite pattern.
Clue 5: She would like a flower in the design.
Clue 6: She wants more than one thing in the design. The dress she chooses is … — D

15. Which of the statements on your sheet is true? — C

16. The moon landing occurred on July 20, 1969. Write this using the short date form. — 7/20/1969

(i) Listen to the clues and pick the shape that matches. Use the letters to answer.

17. I have 2 round faces and a curved surface. — C

18. I have the same number of faces and vertices (corners, points). — B or D

19. All of my faces are exactly the same. — F

20. I have 5 faces and 8 edges. — B

Activity Answers

1. (a) chocolate (b) squid (c) 65 (d) 105 (e) 55

A BLAST OF MATH - BOOK 3 World Teachers Press®

1. _____ 6. _____ 11. _____ 16. _____

2. _____ 7. _____ 12. _____ 17. _____

3. _____ 8. _____ 13. _____ 18. _____

4. _____ 9. _____ 14. _____ 19. _____

5. _____ 10. _____ 15. _____ 20. _____

1
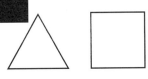

2
A $\frac{1}{2} = \frac{5}{10} = 0.5$

B $\frac{1}{2} = \frac{2}{10} = 0.2$

C $\frac{1}{4} = \frac{4}{10} = 0.4$

3
4 L 200 mL
6 L 750 mL
_____

4–9
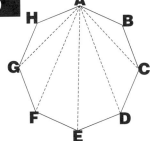

10–12

13
L = _____ cm

W = _____ cm

H = _____ cm

14

A B C D E F G

15
Water boils at

A = 0°C

B = 40° C

C= 100°C

16
July 20, 1969

17–20
A = sphere

B = square pyramid

C = cylinder

D = octagonal pyramid

E = cone

F = cube

Activity

Bar Graph

1. Answer the questions about the bar graph. Note that each square stands for 10 ice-cream cones sold.

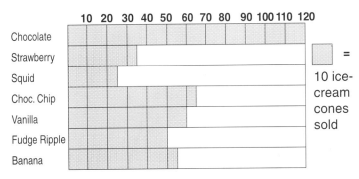

10 20 30 40 50 60 70 80 90 100 110 120

Chocolate
Strawberry
Squid
Choc. Chip
Vanilla
Fudge Ripple
Banana

☐ = 10 ice-cream cones sold

(a) Which flavor was most popular?

_____

(b) Which was least popular?

_____

(c) How many chocolate chip ice-cream cones were sold? _____

(d) What is the combined total of banana and fudge ripple ice-cream cones sold? _____

(e) How many more chocolate than chocolate chip ice-cream cones were sold? _____

BLAST 13

No.	Question and Discussion	Answer
1.	Draw two lines on the shape on your sheet to make it rigid.	AC and AD, BE and BD, or CA and CE
2.	Listen to the clues and eliminate those that don't belong. The number you are left with is the number of teeth an adult has. Clue 1: I'm an even number. Clue 2: I'm less than 2 lots of 20. Clue 3: I'm less than three dozen. Clue 4: Four divides evenly into me. I am …	32

(i) Questions 3 to 7 are about the picture of a cake on your sheet.

No.	Question and Discussion	Answer
3.	Gary wants to eat the frosted pieces. What fraction does he want to eat?	$^7/_{10}$
4.	Write this fraction as a decimal.	0.7
5.	Before he does this, Bruce comes along. He cuts the cake into smaller, equal-sized pieces by cutting from points A to B, C to D, E to F, G to H, I to J, K to L, M to N, O to P and Q to R. Draw cut lines here so you can see what the cake looks like. He eats 22 of the smaller pieces without frosting. What fraction of the cake does he eat?	$^{22}/_{100}$
6.	What fraction of the cake was eaten altogether? **Demonstrate** $^7/_{10} + {}^{22}/_{100} = {}^{70}/_{100} + {}^{22}/_{100} = {}^{92}/_{100}$.	$^{92}/_{100}$
7.	Write the fraction Bruce ate as a decimal.	0.22
8.	If each square on the shaded shape has an area of one square centimeter, what is the area of the shape?	27 cm^2
9.	It is five minutes to 10. Norman's bus comes in eight minutes. Write the time of the bus's arrival using digital notation.	10:03

(i) Use the temperatures given on your sheet to answer the next 6 questions.

No.	Question and Discussion	Answer
10.	Which is the temperature of a piece of ice?	0°C
11.	Which temperature is that of boiling water?	100°C
12.	Which is a good temperature for the food compartment (not the freezer) of your refrigerator?	4°C
13.	Which is a healthy body temperature?	37°C
14.	Which temperature could be that of a very hot summer's day?	42°C
15.	Which temperature not already used could be that of a chilly winter's morning?	10°C
16.	Piece of paper X has been folded into four and cut at the fold point as shown. Which picture shows what it would look like when opened out?	C
17.	Which of the statements for question 17 is true?	B
18.	How many cubes are needed to make the prism on your sheet?	27
19.	What is the volume of the prism on your sheet? Write your answer in cubic centimeters.	56 cm^3
20.	The great Fire of London occurred in the year on your sheet that is in the 17th century. In which year was it?	1666

Activity Answers

1.   (a) 6   (b) 4 and 5   (c) 9   (d) 2   (e) 54   (f) 18

1. _____	6. _____	11. _____	16. _____
2. _____	7. _____	12. _____	17. _____
3. _____	8. _____	13. _____	18. _____
4. _____	9. _____	14. _____	19. _____
5. _____	10. _____	15. _____	20. _____

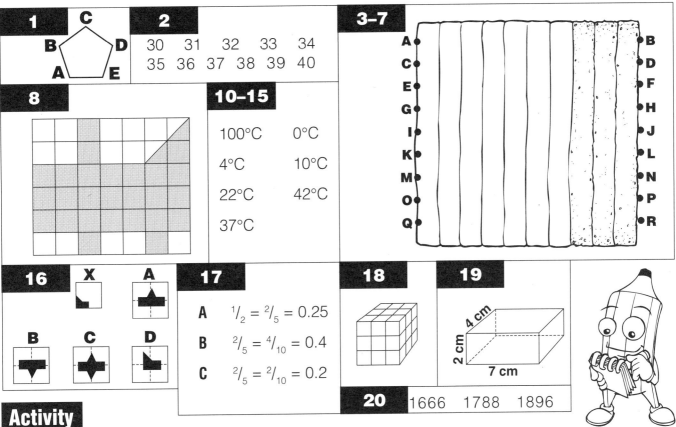

1

2
30 31 32 33 34
35 36 37 38 39 40

3–7

8

10–15
100°C   0°C
4°C   10°C
22°C   42°C
37°C

16   X   A
B   C   D

17
A $^1/_2 = ^2/_5 = 0.25$
B $^2/_5 = ^4/_{10} = 0.4$
C $^2/_5 = ^2/_{10} = 0.2$

18

19   4 cm   2 cm   7 cm

20   1666   1788   1896

Activity

Bar Graph

Book Collection

1. The bar graph shows the number of books collected by the class over twelve days for the "community book club" collection.

   (a) How many books were collected on the first day? _____

   (b) On what day/days were the most books collected? _____

   (c) On what day/days were the least books collected? _____

   (d) What was the most common number of books collected per day? _____

   (e) What was the total number of books collected? _____

   (f) How many books were collected in total on days 4, 7, 9 and 12? _____

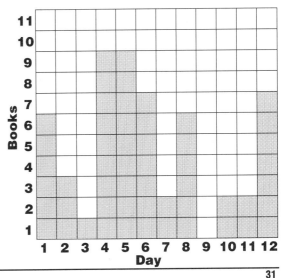

BLAST 14

No.	Question and Discussion	Answer
1.	Write the numeral for the number shown by the abacus.	74,653
2.	Draw three more beads on the units bar and one more on the tens of thousands bar. Write the numeral for the new number shown.	84,656
3.	An Olympic runner takes about 10 seconds to run the 100 meters sprint. How long will it take him to run the 1,000 meters in a one kilometer race? Choose A, B, or C.	B

It is impossible to sustain 100 m speed over a kilometer.

Listen to the clues and write the letter or letters from those given that fits the description.

No.	Question and Discussion	Answer
4.	Name any two shapes that look the same from a top view.	C and D
5.	Which two shapes have one round face and one curved surface?	B and D
6.	Which shape is like a wizard's hat?	B
7.	Which shape is like a drum?	C
8.	What is the area of the rectangle represented on your sheet?	18 m^2
9.	Which statement on your sheet for question 9 is true?	C
10.	Add the two capacities on your sheet, then write the total on answer line 10.	9 L 850 mL
11.	Listen and write down the measurements of this rectangular prism. Work out its volume in cubic centimeters and write it on the answer line. Length = 5 cm Width = 6 cm Height = 10 cm	300 cm^3
12.	Are the three lengths on your sheet all the same?	no

Use decimal notation to write 532 centimeters as meters. Follow the steps as I say them.

No.	Question and Discussion	Answer
13.	Write the number of whole meters in 532 centimeters. Put a decimal point to separate whole meters from parts of a meter. Write the remaining centimeters after the decimal point and put "m" for "meters" at the end.	5.32 m
14.	Write the largest four digit numeral you can using the four digits.	7,431
15.	Now write the smallest four digit numeral you can using them.	1,347
16.	If today is Tuesday, what day is it two days after yesterday? Choose from the abbreviations.	Wed.
17.	If a person was born on the 1st January 1956, how old would they be today?	teacher
18.	What would the area of the shaded triangle formed by the diagonal be?	10 m^2
19.	Circle the numeral in the thousands column on the answer line.	7
20.	Circle the numeral in the tens of thousands column on the answer line.	6

Activity Answers

1.   (a) 500   (b) 750   (c) 1,000   (d) 1,250   (e) 1,500   (f) 1,750   (g) 2,000   (h) 2,250

1. _____ 6. _____ 11. _____ 16. _____

2. _____ 7. _____ 12. _____ 17. _____

3. _____ 8. _____ 13. _____ 18. _____

4. _____ 9. _____ 14. _____ 19. 3 7,4 2 5

5. _____ 10. _____ 15. _____ 20. 6 2,3 5 7

1–2

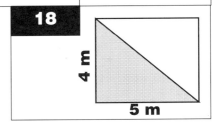

10th   th   h   t   u

3

A = 100 sec

B = more than 100 sec

C = less than 100 sec but more than 10 sec

4–7

A = pentagonal prism

B = cone

C = cylinder

D = hemisphere

E = triangular prism

8

3 m × 6 m

9

A $\frac{1}{2} = \frac{2}{4} = 2.4$

B $\frac{3}{5} = \frac{6}{10} = 0.3$

C $\frac{2}{5} = \frac{4}{10} = 0.4$

10

3 L 450 mL
6 L 400 mL
_____

11

L = _____ cm
W = _____ cm
H = _____ cm

12

350 cm
$3\frac{1}{2}$ cm
3.5 cm

14–15

4 7 1 3

16

Mon. Tues.
Wed. Thurs.

18

4 m × 5 m triangle

Activity   Multiplying by multiples of 25

Do the addition below. In each case you are adding 25 sets of the same number. Write answers in the answer spaces and then next to the multiplication number sentences. Can you make up a rule that works for these multiplications?

A	B	C	D	E	F	G	H
20	30	40	50	60	70	80	90
20	30	40	50	60	70	80	90
20	30	40	50	60	70	80	90
20	30	40	50	60	70	80	90
20	30	40	50	60	70	80	90
20	30	40	50	60	70	80	90
20	30	40	50	60	70	80	90
20	30	40	50	60	70	80	90
20	30	40	50	60	70	80	90
20	30	40	50	60	70	80	90
20	30	40	50	60	70	80	90
20	30	40	50	60	70	80	90
20	30	40	50	60	70	80	90
20	30	40	50	60	70	80	90
20	30	40	50	60	70	80	90
20	30	40	50	60	70	80	90
20	30	40	50	60	70	80	90
20	30	40	50	60	70	80	90
20	30	40	50	60	70	80	90
20	30	40	50	60	70	80	90
20	30	40	50	60	70	80	90
20	30	40	50	60	70	80	90
20	30	40	50	60	70	80	90
+ 20	+ 30	+ 40	+ 50	+ 60	+ 70	+ 80	+ 90

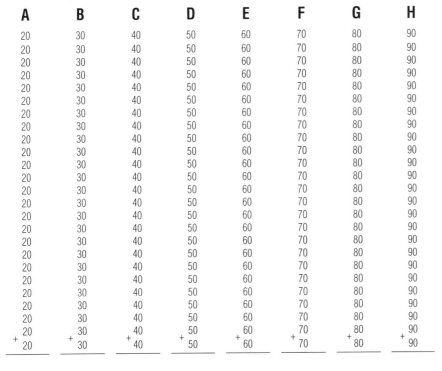

Number sentences

(a) 25 x 20 = _____

(b) 25 x 30 = _____

(c) 25 x 40 = _____

(d) 25 x 50 = _____

(e) 25 x 60 = _____

(f) 25 x 70 = _____

(g) 25 x 80 = _____

(h) 25 x 90 = _____

BLAST 15

No.	Question and Discussion	Answer
1.	What is the area of the rectangular garden on your sheet?	160 m²
2.	Ron is celebrating his 45th birthday. Which birthday will he be celebrating 150 years from now?	neither
	People don't live long enough for Ron to be celebrating anything in 150 years' time.	
3.	What year will it be 75 years from this year?	teacher
4.	Use one of the letters to answer this question. If a right-handed glove is turned inside out, which of the possibilities does it become?	B
5.	Which of the statements for question 5 is true?	A

> ⓘ Questions 6 to 10 relate to the road sign on your sheet. It shows the distance between 5 Australian towns. All distances are in kilometers.

No.	Question and Discussion	Answer
6.	How far is it from Swan Hill to Lake Boga?	15 km
7.	How far is it from Kerang to Cohuna?	35 km
8.	How far is it from Lake Boga to Cohuna?	80 km
9.	How far is it from Gunbower to Cohuna?	17 km
10.	Imagine that you are in the car approaching the sign. The car is traveling at the speed of 100 kilometers per hour. About how long will it take to get to Swan Hill? Choose from the times on your sheet.	10 min
11.	Write the next number in Pattern A.	72,460
12.	Write the next number in Pattern B.	75,250
13.	Today's date is _____. Write this using short form.	teacher
14.	Draw a diagonal from A to C. What would the area of triangle ABC be?	14 m²
15.	A gram of rice is made up of 75 grains. How many grains would there be in a kilogram?	75,000

> ⓘ The last 5 questions relate to the picture showing top, front and side views. Write "front," "top," or "side" to answer.

No.	Question and Discussion	Answer
16.	Which view of the car is shown in A?	side
17.	Which view of Larry is shown in F?	top
18.	Which view of the ship does I show?	front
19.	Which view of the car does C show?	front
20.	Which view of Larry does E show?	side

Activity Answers

1. (a) E   (b) C   (c) A   (d) B   (e) F   (f) D

1. _____   6. _____   11. _____   16. _____

2. _____   7. _____   12. _____   17. _____

3. _____   8. _____   13. _____   18. _____

4. _____   9. _____   14. _____   19. _____

5. _____   10. _____   15. _____   20. _____

1

20 m

8 m

2

150th

195th

neither

4

A = right-handed

B = left-handed

5

A $\quad {}^{2}/_{20} = {}^{1}/_{10} = 0.1$

B $\quad {}^{2}/_{20} = {}^{1}/_{40} = 0.4$

C $\quad {}^{2}/_{20} = {}^{4}/_{10} = 0.4$

6–10

Swan Hill	10
Lake Boga	25
Kerang	70
Cohuna	105
Gunbower	122

| 45 min | 10 min |
| 1 min | $1^{1}/_{2}$ hrs |

11–12

| A | 72,160 | 72,260 | 72,360 | ? |
| B | 45,250 | 55,250 | 65,250 | ? |

16–20 Front   Top   Side

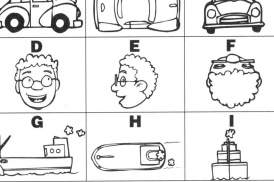

A   B   C

D   E   F

G   H   I

14

A   D

4 m

B   C
      7 m

Activity

Nets of 3-D shapes

1. Match the nets with their 3-D shapes by writing the letters.

    (a) Which is the net of a square pyramid? _____

    (b) Which is the net of a triangular pyramid? _____

    (c) Which is the net of a triangular prism? _____

    (d) Which is the net of a rectangular prism? _____

    (e) Which is the net of a cube? _____

    (f) Which is the net of a cylinder? _____

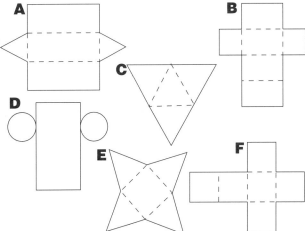

A   B   C   D   E   F

BLAST 16

No.	Question and Discussion	Answer
1.	Add the two volumes on your sheet then write the answer on the answer line.	6 L 250 mL
2.	Vanessa catches the school bus at 8:45 a.m. and arrives at the school gate at 9:20 a.m. What length of time is she on the bus?	35 min
3.	Write 1:30 p.m. in 24-hour time.	13:30

24-hour time starts at midnight. When 12 noon is reached, hours are just added on. 1:00 p.m. becomes 13:00 (13 hundred), 2:00 p.m. becomes 14:00 (14 hundred), etc. This time is used by the armed forces, at airports, etc.

No.	Question and Discussion	Answer
4.	Are 150 mL, 1.5 L and $1\frac{1}{2}$ liters all the same amount?	no
5.	What comes next in number pattern A?	5.5
6.	What comes next in number pattern B?	5.8
7.	Which amount is most likely to be the capacity of a car's gas tank?	70 L
8.	Which statement for question 8 is true?	A

(i) Questions 9 to 13 are about the picture of a cake on your sheet.

No.	Question and Discussion	Answer
9.	Katie wants to eat the frosted pieces. What fraction of the cake does she want to eat?	$\frac{3}{20}$
10.	Before she eats this, Audrey comes along. She cuts the cake into smaller, equal-sized pieces by cutting from A to B, C to D, E to F and G to H. Draw cut lines here so that you can see what the cake looks like. She eats 19 of the smaller pieces without frosting. What fraction does she eat?	$\frac{19}{100}$
11.	What fraction of the cake was eaten altogether?	$\frac{34}{100}$

Demonstrate $\frac{3}{20} + \frac{19}{100} = \frac{15}{100} + \frac{19}{100} = \frac{34}{100}$.

No.	Question and Discussion	Answer
12.	Write the fraction that Audrey ate as a decimal.	0.19
13.	Write the fraction both girls ate together as a decimal.	0.34
14.	A man is painting a room. Look at the picture. As you can see, he is working backwards toward the door. Unfortunately, when he is three steps from the door he steps into some paint he is using. Whenever he puts his foot down, it leaves a painted footprint mark. How many footprints will be left on the floor of the room when he has finished painting it?	0

When he has finished the painting, any footprints on the unpainted section will be painted over. Since he stepped in the paint he was using, there would be no traces of any footprints.

No.	Question and Discussion	Answer
15.	What is the area of field WXYZ?	3,200 m²
16.	Draw a diagonal from W to Z. What is the area of triangle WXZ?	1,600 m²

(i) The last 4 questions are about the top views on your sheet.

No.	Question and Discussion	Answer
17.	Which picture shows the top view of a pentagonal prism?	A
18.	Which picture shows the top view of a pentagonal pyramid?	C
19.	Which picture shows the top view of an octagonal prism?	B
20.	Which picture shows the top view of an octagonal pyramid?	D

Activity Answers

1. (a) obtuse   (b) reflex   (c) right   (d) acute   (e) straight

1. _____   6. _____   11. _____   16. _____

2. _____   7. _____   12. _____   17. _____

3. _____   8. _____   13. _____   18. _____

4. _____   9. _____   14. _____   19. _____

5. _____   10. _____   15. _____   20. _____

1

3 L 750 mL
2 L 500 mL
_____

4

150 mL   1.5 mL   1½ L

5

A = 1.5   2.5   3.5   4.5   ?

6

B = 0.3   1.4   2.5   3.6   4.7   ?

7

7 L   70 L   700 L   7,000 L

8

A $^{18}/_{20} = {}^9/_{10} = 0.9$

B $^9/_{10} = {}^4/_5 = 0.8$

C $^{18}/_{20} = {}^9/_{40} = 0.3$

9–13

= frosted

14

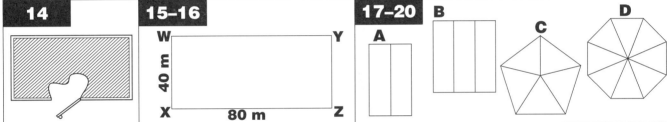

15–16

W _____ Y
40 m
X ___80 m___ Z

17–20   A   B   C   D

Activity

Angles

1. Work out the answers, then write the code letter to name the type of angle.

   (a) Angle ABC is an ____ ____ ____ ____ ____ ____ angle.
   4x4   7-4   3x7   2x11   5x4   3+3

   (b) Angle CDE is a ____ ____ ____ ____ ____ ____ angle.
   11+8   4+2   4+3   6+7   1+5   5x5

   (c) Angle DEF is a ____ ____ ____ ____ ____ angle.
   20-1   2x5   4x2   3x3   7x3

   (d) Angle KLM is an ____ ____ ____ ____ ____ angle.
   6-4   2x2   11x2   15+6   10-4

   (e) Angle MNO is a ____ ____ ____ ____ ____ ____ ____ angle.
   4x5   19+2   0+19   3-1   5x2   5+3   6+3   15+6

CODE	
a = 2	n = 15
b = 3	o = 16
c = 4	p = 17
d = 5	q = 18
e = 6	r = 19
f = 7	s = 20
g = 8	t = 21
h = 9	u = 22
i = 10	v = 23
j = 11	w = 24
k = 12	x = 25
l = 13	y = 26
m = 14	z = 27

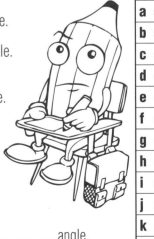

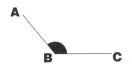
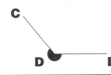

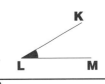

No.	Question and Discussion	Answer
1.	Circle the temperature on the answer line that shows a healthy body temperature.	37°C
(i)	The next 3 questions are about the circles on your sheet. Use the code to work out the name of the part labeled on each.	
2.		circumference
3.		diameter
4.		radius
5.	April Fool's Day falls on the first day of April. Write the short date of April Fool's Day this year.	teacher
6.	Colin buys some wood and nails for $13.00 and builds a dog kennel. He sells it for $23.00. What is his profit?	$10.00
7.	Brent collects coins. He goes into a dealer's shop. The dealer shows him three coins: an English coin dated 1723, an Australian coin dated 1996 and a coin from Ancient Rome dated 55 BC. The dealer has a reputation for dishonesty and Brent knows he deserves it because one of the coins is definitely a fake. Which one?	55 BC
(i)	Jim has decided to go searching for the long lost treasure of Captain Bluebeard, the ferocious pirate. Listen carefully to where he swims and write where he finishes. The words can be found in the word bank.	
8.	From C7 he swims four down and three right. What does he bump into?	octopus
9.	From G6 he swims two down, six left and three down. What does he get tangled up in?	seaweed
10.	From D1 he swims two up and two left. What chases him away angrily?	crab
11.	From A7 he swims five down, four right and one down. What does he stumble over?	treasure
12.	From E1 he swims six up, one left and one up. Where does he finish?	boat
13.	Which amount on your sheet is the same as a quarter of a kilogram?	250 g
(i)	The next 4 questions are about side views of common 3-D shapes.	
14.	Which side view could be a cylinder?	A
15.	Which side view could be a sphere?	B
16.	Which side view could be an octagonal prism?	D
17.	Which side view could be a hexagonal prism?	C
18.	What is the area of the triangle on your sheet?	24 m²
19.	A number is a factor of another number if it divides into it evenly (i.e., without any remainder). Circle the number on your answer line that is not a factor of 20.	8
20.	Write this information on your sheet, then work out the answer. A rectangular prism has a length of 2 cm, a width of 3 cm and a height of 9 cm. What is its volume in cubic centimeters?	54 cm³

Activity Answers

1.   (a) 4   (b) 9   (c) 16   (d) 25

1. 0°C   37°C   100°C   6. _____   11. _____   16. _____

2. A = _____   7. _____   12. _____   17. _____

3. B = _____   8. _____   13. _____   18. _____

4. C = _____   9. _____   14. _____   19. 1 2 4 8 10 20

5. _____   10. _____   15. _____   20. _____

2–4

A _____

3^2 19+6 7^2 4+5   8x7 6^2 9+8 4^2 7x7   8x2   8x5   5+4   4x4

B _____

5x2 5^2 2^2 4x9   9+7   6x9   8+8   50-1

C _____

7^2 8-4   2x5   5x5   7x8   5x10

7   **1723**

1996   **55 BC**

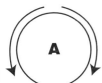

A = 4   B = 5   C = 9   D = 10   E = 16   F = 17
G = 18   H = 20   I = 25   J = 26   K = 27   L = 28
M = 36   N = 40   O = 42   P = 44   Q = 45   R = 49
S = 50   T = 54   U = 56   V = 60   W = 61   X = 62
Y = 63   Z = 64

8–12

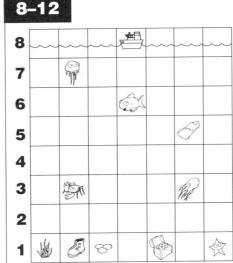

3 stones
fish
treasure
octopus
jellyfish
seaweed
old boot
flipper
crab
starfish
boat

13

25 g
250 g
2,500 g

14–17

A   B   C   D

18

8 m

6 m

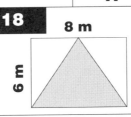

20   **Working**

Length = _____
Width = _____
Height = _____

Activity   *Square numbers*

1. Make square patterns from the square numbers. Remember, when you square a number, you multiply it by itself.

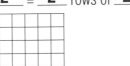   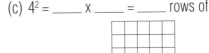

(a) 2^2 = **2** x **2** = **2** rows of **2** = **4**   (c) 4^2 = _____ x _____ = _____ rows of _____ = _____

(b) 3^2 = _____ x _____ = _____ rows of _____ = _____   (d) 5^2 = _____ x _____ = _____ rows of _____ = _____

BLAST 18

No.	Question and Discussion	Answer

1. Which of the measurements on your sheet is the same as a quarter of a meter? — 25 cm

2. Joy, Felicity and Gracie Mouse are hungrily looking at the two cakes on the sheet. Each cake is cut up into five equal-sized pieces. They decide that each should have three slices of cake. What fraction of a cake does each mouse eat? — $^3/_5$

> *Note that the two cakes are separate whole cakes. Each slice is equal to $^1/_5$ of one cake. Make children aware of this, otherwise some may think that each slice is equal to $^1/_{10}$ of a cake.*

3. Shade each mouse's share a different color. Do they eat more than one whole cake altogether? — yes

4. What amount of cake was eaten altogether? Your answer should have a whole number and a fraction part in it. — $1^4/_5$

> *A fraction made up of a whole number and a fraction part is called a "mixed numeral" ("mixed" because it is a mixture of a whole number and a fraction). The same fraction could be written $^9/_5$. Written this way it is called an "improper fraction."*

> (i) Listen carefully to the information. You will have to write down some numbers to work out the answer to a question.

5. What was the total attendance on the first two days of the 1999 World Series? On the first day 9,119 people attended. On the second day 17,277 people attended. Now work out the total and write it on answer line 5. — 26,396

6. Using your ruler and different colored pencils, draw lines to construct the angles named. After constructing the angle, write the type that it is using words from the word bank. Construct angle EOM. What type is it? — right

7. Construct angle DHI. What type is it on the inside? — acute

8. Construct angle UVW. What type of angle is it? — straight

9. Construct angle FQR. What type of angle is it on the inside? — obtuse

10. What type of angle does FQR make on the outside? — reflex

11. How many blocks were used to make the solid on your sheet? — 32

12. Write 20 past 6 in the evening in 24-hour time. — 18:20

13. What is the smallest number of coins you can use to make $5.55? You can use each coin more than once. — $1.00 x 5, 50¢, 5¢

14. Write $1.67 rounded to the nearest 10¢. — $1.70

15. The owner of a sports store buys softball bats for $29.00. She sells them for $47.00. How much profit does she make on a bat? — $18.00

16. Which front view matches the isometric drawing? — B

> *Isometric drawings are used to show models of 3-D shapes. They are drawn using 3 axes. The axis showing height is drawn vertically. The other axes are drawn at an angle to this (usually 30 degrees).*

17. Which of the statements for question 17 is true? — C

> *Note that "percent" comes from the Latin "per centum" meaning "out of 100." "Sixty percent" means 60 out of 100.*

18. Farmer Brown has pigs and geese in one field. There are six heads and sixteen feet. How many geese are there? Experiment by drawing in the empty field on your answer sheet. — 4 geese (2 pigs)

19. The incomplete word on the line has all its vowels missing. It means the distance around the outside of something. Put in the missing vowels to complete the word. — perimeter

20. There are 20 weeds in Graham's garden. He says he is going to pull them out in three days, pulling an odd number every day. Is it possible for him to do this? — no

> *An odd number of odd numbers always give an odd number as their total.*

Additional Material Needed

Each child needs a ruler and colored pencils

Activity Answers

1.   (a) 6   (b) 5   (c) sandwiches   (d) 6   (e) 35

1. _____   6. _____   11. _____   16. _____

2. _____   7. _____   12. _____   17. _____

3. _____   8. _____   13. _____   18. _____

4. _____   9. _____   14. _____   19. p__r__m__t__r

5. _____   10. _____   15. _____   20. _____

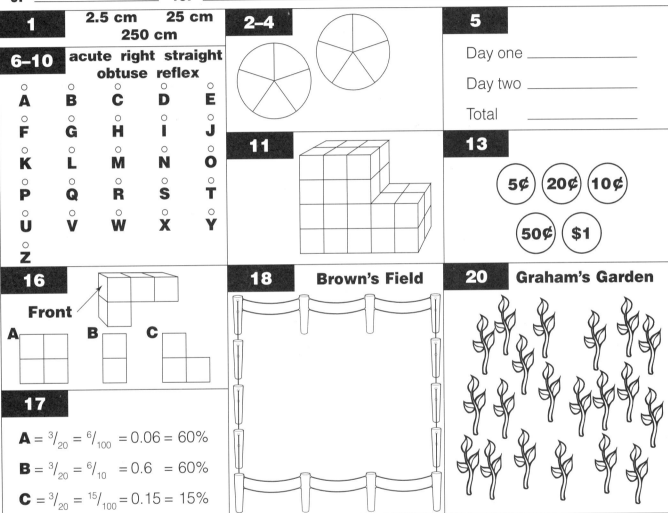

1 2.5 cm   25 cm   250 cm

6–10 acute right straight obtuse reflex

○ A   ○ B   ○ C   ○ D   ○ E
○ F   ○ G   ○ H   ○ I   ○ J
○ K   ○ L   ○ M   ○ N   ○ O
○ P   ○ Q   ○ R   ○ S   ○ T
○ U   ○ V   ○ W   ○ X   ○ Y
○ Z

2–4

11

16 Front A B C

17

$A = \frac{3}{20} = \frac{6}{100} = 0.06 = 60\%$

$B = \frac{3}{20} = \frac{6}{10} = 0.6 = 60\%$

$C = \frac{3}{20} = \frac{15}{100} = 0.15 = 15\%$

5 Day one _____ Day two _____ Total _____

13 5¢ 20¢ 10¢ 50¢ $1

18 Brown's Field

20 Graham's Garden

Activity

Bar Graphs

1. The bar graph shows what children in room 5A had for lunch one day. The number of things eaten is written along the bottom in this bar graph. Bar graphs can have bars running either vertically (up and down) or horizontally (across).

   (a) How many children had veggie burgers? _____

   (b) How many had hamburgers? _____

   (c) What was the most popular lunch? _____

   (d) How many more had chef's salad than pizza? _____

   (e) How many children are there in room 5A? _____

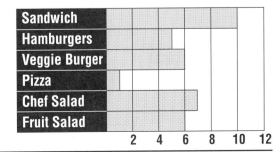

	2	4	6	8	10	12
Sandwich						
Hamburgers						
Veggie Burger						
Pizza						
Chef Salad						
Fruit Salad						

BLAST 19

No.	Question and Discussion	Answer
1.	Farmer Blue has cows and ducks in a field. There are 7 heads and 26 feet. How many ducks are there? Experiment by drawing in the field on your sheet.	1 duck (6 cows)
	Allow 1 minute for working.	
2.	Listen to the clues and find out where the Bloggs family spent their vacation. Eliminate places that don't belong as you hear the clues.	
	CLUE 1: It isn't the most southerly place.	
	CLUE 2: It isn't on a bay.	
	CLUE 3: It's not the closest place to the mountains.	
	CLUE 4: It's not the resort 20 kilometers from Hillview.	
	CLUE 5: It's north of Middleton. They went to …	Hypeton
3.	Circle the number on answer line 3 that isn't a factor of 24.	5
4.	Write any equivalent fraction of $\frac{1}{4}$.	teacher
5.	Add the volumes on your sheet, then write the answer on answer line 5.	6 L 750 mL
6.	Polly put the kettle on at 5 minutes to 10 one morning. She took it off again 12 minutes later. Using a.m. or p.m., write what time it was when she took it off.	10:07 a.m.
7.	Write 25 past 10 at night using 24-hour time.	22:25
8.	What is the area of a rectangle with a length of 7 meters and a width of 5 meters?	35 m^2
9.	The "product" is the answer you get when you multiply. What is the product of 7 and 5?	35
10.	Which picture on your sheet matches the front view of the isometric drawing?	B
11.	Draw the rhombus on your answer line as it would look if flipped.	teacher

ⓘ The next 5 questions are about the problem on your sheet.

No.	Question and Discussion	Answer
12.	Read aloud with the class. What are we trying to find out? Listen carefully, then answer A, B, or C. A = How old Sean is. B = How much older Sean is than Shamus. C = Which leprechaun is older.	B
13.	Which operations symbol would you use to find the answer?	−
14.	Use the working space to find the answer, then write it on answer line 14.	13 yrs
15.	Use the working space to find the next 2 answers. As you know, leprechauns live to great ages. Both Sean and Shamus are still alive. They were both born on the first of January. How old is Sean now?	teacher
16.	How old is Shamus now?	teacher
17.	Which of the answers for question 17 equals a quarter of a meter?	0.25 m

ⓘ The last 3 questions are about Bartholomew Butterfly.

No.	Question and Discussion	Answer
18.	In which picture has he been flipped?	A
19.	In which picture has he been slid?	B
20.	In which picture has he been turned?	C

Activity Answers

1.
(a) 40	(d) 50	(g) 90	(j) 0
(b) 70	(e) 30	(h) 50	
(c) 40	(f) 10	(i) 100	

1. _____   6. _____   11. 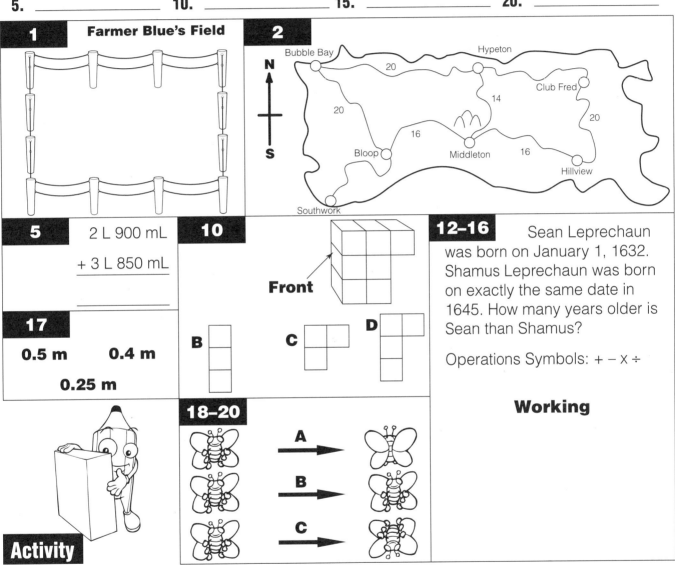   16. _____

2. _____   7. _____   12. _____   17. _____

3. **1 2 3 4 5 6**   8. _____   13. _____   18. _____

4. _____   9. _____   14. _____   19. _____

5. _____   10. _____   15. _____   20. _____

1 Farmer Blue's Field

2

N / S

Bubble Bay 20 Hypeton Club Fred
20 14 20
16 Middleton 16
Bloop Hillview
Southwork

5   2 L 900 mL
+ 3 L 850 mL
_____

17
0.5 m   0.4 m
0.25 m

10   Front

B   **C**   **D**

12–16   Sean Leprechaun was born on January 1, 1632. Shamus Leprechaun was born on exactly the same date in 1645. How many years older is Sean than Shamus?

Operations Symbols: + − x ÷

Working

Activity

18–20

A
B
C

Rounding

When rounding to the nearest 10, numbers ending in 1, 2, 3, or 4 are rounded back to the same number of tens. Numbers ending in 5, 6, 7, 8, or 9 are rounded "up" to the next ten.

Example: 22 = 20 to the nearest ten, but 25 = 30 to the nearest ten.

1.   Round these numbers to the nearest ten:

(a) 37 _____   (c) 43 _____   (e) 29 _____   (g) 87 _____   (i) 95 _____

(b) 74 _____   (d) 54 _____   (f) 11 _____   (h) 49 _____   (j) 4 _____

No.	Question and Discussion	Answer
1.	Which statement for question 1 is true?	A
2.	Which amount given for question 2 equals a quarter of a liter?	0.25 L
3.	Which front view matches the isometric drawing?	B
4.	Unscramble the letters to make the word that means the answer we get when we multiply.	product
5.	If each square on the shaded shape has an area of one square centimeter, what is the area of the shape?	18 cm^2
6.	Roma wants to eat the frosted portion of the cake on your sheet. What fraction of the cake does she want to eat?	$^2/_5$
7.	Before she can do this, Lesley comes along and cuts the cake up differently. Draw lines to show how she cuts the cake. She cuts from A to B, C to D, then E to F. She then eats seven of the newly cut pieces. What fraction does she eat?	$^7/_{20}$
8.	What fraction of the cake was eaten altogether?	$^{15}/_{20}$
9.	Change $^2/_5$ into tenths by multiplying the top and bottom numbers by two.	$^4/_{10}$

With enough experience showing how fractions can be changed to equivalents by cutting differently, children should be ready to accept the shortcut – i.e., multiplying the numerator and denominator by the same amount.

No.	Question and Discussion	Answer
10.	Change $^7/_{20}$ into hundredths by multiplying top and bottom by five.	$^{35}/_{100}$
11.	Circle the number on the answer line that isn't a factor of 18.	4
12.	Write down the information to work out this problem in the working space on your sheet. There were 736 students at the high school. Only 188 were boys. How many were girls?	548
13.	Is it cheaper for mom to take two children to the circus at once or to take them separately?	A

Mom only has to pay for herself once.

No.	Question and Discussion	Answer
14.	Which word in the word bank means the answer when we add?	total
15.	Which means the answer when we subtract?	difference
16.	Which means the answer when we divide?	quotient
17.	What is the perimeter of a square with sides five meters long?	20 m
18.	What is the area of the same square?	25 m^2
19.	Liam wakes up at 18 minutes to seven one morning. Write this time in figures.	6:42 a.m.
20.	Write the time 20 minutes after this.	7:02 a.m.

Activity Answers

1. (a) 9:55 a.m.
   (b) 10:30 p.m.
   (c) 1 hr 15 mins
   (d) Colby and Black Rock
   (e) 17 hours

1. _____   6. _____   11. **1 2 3 4**   16. _____

2. _____   7. _____   12. _____   17. _____

3. _____   8. _____   13. _____   18. _____

4. _____   9. _____   14. _____   19. _____

5. _____   10. _____   15. _____   20. _____

1

$A = \frac{9}{20} = \frac{45}{100} = 0.45 = 45\%$

$B = \frac{9}{20} = \frac{18}{100} = 0.18 = 18\%$

$C = \frac{9}{20} = \frac{90}{100} = 0.9 = 90\%$

2

0.25 L	0.25 mL	1.4 L

4

r   p   t   d   c   u   o

3

← **Front**

A

B   D

C

5

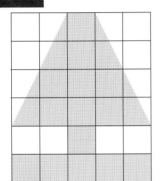

6–10

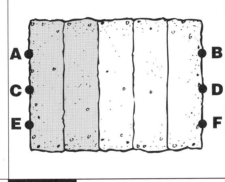

A   B

C   D

E   F

12

Students _____

Girls _____

Boys _____

13

A = both at once

B = separately

14–16

product   total

difference   quotient

17–18

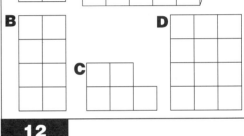

5 m

5 m

Activity

Schedules

Answer the questions about the train schedule.

1. The times have been written in 24-hour time. Convert back to a.m. or p.m. when you write your answers.

    (a) When does the train arrive at Leedale? _____

    (b) When does it arrive at Black Rock? _____

    (c) How long does the trip from Black Rock to Sand City take? _____

    (d) Which two adjacent stops are probably furthest apart? _____

    (e) How long does the trip from Newbury to Sand City take? _____

TRAIN SCHEDULE	
Newbury	06:45
Leedale	09:55
Linden	11:30
Hansbrook	13:05
Castorp	14:55
Colby	18:40
Black Rock	22:30
Sand City	23:45

BLAST 21

No.	Question and Discussion	Answer

ℹ️ Refer to the groups of marbles on your sheet to answer questions 1 to 5. Notice that each group has the same number of marbles in it and also the same number colored and clear.

1. How many marbles are in each group? — 5

2. How many marbles in each group are colored? — 3

3. What fraction of each group is colored? — $^3/_5$

4. If you count groups A, B, C, D, E and F as one big group, what fraction of marbles in this big group is colored? — $^{18}/_{30}$

5. How many is $^3/_5$ of 30? — 18

> *Show children how this is done using the shortcut method. $^3/_5$ x 30 = divide 30 by the denominator (30 ÷ 5 = 6) and multiply the answer by the numerator (6 x 3 = 18).*

6. Circle the three numbers on answer line 6 that aren't factors of 11. — 2, 3, 5

> *Note that 11 is a "prime number." A prime number is only divisible by itself and one. Its only factors, therefore, are itself and one.*

7. Which of the areas given for question 7 is closest to that of the average school classroom? — 30 m²

8. Which of the decimals given for question 8 means 15 hundredths? — 0.15

9. Which mass for question 9 means a quarter of a ton? — 0.25 t

10. Which statement for question 10 is true? — C

11. To find the average, you must divide the total by the number of scores. In three quarters for the school basketball team, Vince scores a total of 30 points. What is his average score per quarter? — 10

12. John doesn't roll his socks into pairs after washing them. He just throws them into the drawer all mixed up. He has 20 socks altogether, 10 red and 10 white. One day when his drawer became stuck, he couldn't see the socks. He could only just fit his fingers in to pull out one sock at a time. What is the smallest number of socks he could pull out to be absolutely sure that he has a pair of the same color? — 3

ℹ️ Questions 13 to 15 are about the priceless family portrait of Reggie Rabbit.

13. In which picture has the priceless portrait been flipped? — B

14. In which has it been slid? — A

15. In which has it been turned? — C

16. Which calculator button do you use to find the product of 2 numbers? — x

17. Which would you use to find the quotient? — ÷

18. Which do you use to find the difference? — −

19. Which month spelled backwards is a vegetable? — May = yam

20. Work out the volume on your sheet, then write the answer on line 20. — 7 L 500 mL

Activity Answers

1. (a) Britain and India
(b) 140
(c) 35
(d) 610

1. _____
2. _____
3. _____
4. _____
5. _____

6. 1 2 3 5 11
7. _____
8. _____
9. _____
10. _____

11. _____
12. _____
13. _____
14. _____
15. _____

16. _____
17. _____
18. _____
19. _____
20. _____

1–5					

7	2 m²	2 cm²
	200 m²	30 m²

9		
0.25 t	0.4 t	0.25 kg

11	To find the average, you must divide the total by the number of scores.

8	0.015 0.15
	1.500 15.0

10	
A	$^{13}/_{20}$ = $^{13}/_{100}$ = 0.13 = 13%
B	$^{13}/_{20}$ = $^{26}/_{100}$ = 0.26 = 26%
C	$^{13}/_{20}$ = $^{65}/_{100}$ = 0.65 = 65%

13–15

Painted by Arthur Scribbler

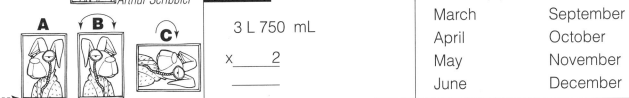

A   B   C

16–18	+ − X ÷

20	3 L 750 mL
	x _____2
	_____

19   **Names of Months**

January	July
February	August
March	September
April	October
May	November
June	December

Activity

Bar Graph

1. Lloyd has made a bar graph to show the number of stamps he has from each country.

   (a) From which two countries does he have the same number of stamps? _____

   (b) How many Australian stamps does he have? _____

   (c) How many Polish stamps does he have? _____

   (d) How many stamps does he have altogether? Use the working space to find the answer. _____

   Working

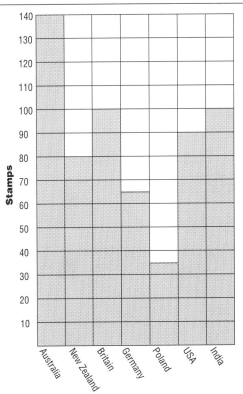

BLAST 22

No.	Question and Discussion	Answer
1.	If 100 plus 63 is 163, how much is 99 plus 63?	162
2.	If 100 plus 36 is 136, how much is 98 plus 36?	134
3.	Piece of paper X has been folded and cut as shown by the shaded area. What does the cut area look like when the paper is unfolded?	C
4.	Which front view matches the isometric drawing?	C
5.	How many whole squares are contained in the shape?	10
6.	How many parts that are a half square or more are contained by the shape?	8
7.	Add these together to find the approximate number of squares the shape contains.	18

Point out that this is the method commonly used to estimate the area of irregular shapes (i.e., wholes and halves or greater are counted, areas less than a half are ignored).

(*i*) Refer to the groups of marbles to answer questions 8 to 12. Notice that each group has the same number of marbles in it and also the same number colored and clear.

No.	Question and Discussion	Answer
8.	How many marbles are in each group?	3
9.	How many in each group are colored?	2
10.	What fraction of each group is colored?	$^2/_3$
11.	How many is $^2/_3$ of 36?	24
12.	What fraction of all the groups combined is clear?	$^{12}/_{36}$ or $^1/_3$
13.	Which of the heights given is closest to that of the ceiling of an average house?	B
14.	Which temperature is closest to that of an air-conditioned room?	20°C
15.	How many centimeters in 1 meter?	100 cm
16.	How many centimeters in 9 meters?	900 cm
17.	How many centimeters in 9.65 meters?	965 cm

18.–19. Choose a child to flip a coin 10 times. Ask the children to predict the number of times it will fall heads or tails. Tally results on the lines provided and write the total number on answers lines 18 and 19. teacher

Point out that in the long term the difference between the two results should be negligible.

No.	Question and Discussion	Answer
20.	Which match has to be moved to change capital "C" to capital "Z?"	2

Additional Material Needed

A coin for flipping

Activity Answers

1.   (a) 16   (b) 17   (c) 2   (d) 5th   (d) yes

1. _____   6. _____   11. _____   16. _____

2. _____   7. _____   12. _____   17. _____

3. _____   8. _____   13. _____   18. Heads = _____

4. _____   9. _____   14. _____   19. Tails = _____

5. _____   10. _____   15. _____   20. _____

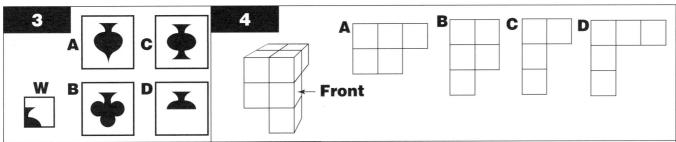

3

A   C   W   B   D

4   Front   A   B   C   D

5–7

8–12

A   B   C   D   E   F   G   H   I   J   K   L

13

A   10 m to 15 m

B $2\frac{1}{2}$ m to $3\frac{1}{2}$ m

C   5 m to 10 m

D $10\frac{1}{2}$ m to $11\frac{1}{2}$ m

14

4°C   20°C

35°C   50°C

15–17

9.65m

18–19

Heads _____

Tails _____

20

1   2   3

Activity

Line Graphs

1. The line graph shows Leah's scores out of 20 in her class's math tests. Altogether the class has had ten tests this year.

   (a) What was her score in the first test? _____

   (b) What was her score in her fourth test? _____

   (c) How many times did she get no mistakes? _____

   (d) Leah was away one day and missed a test.

   Which test was this? _____

   (e) Do you think Leah is good at math? _____

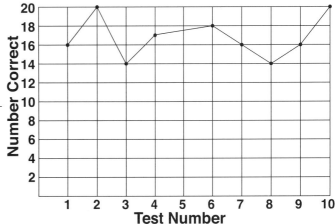

BLAST 23

No.	Question and Discussion	Answer
1.	How many whole squares does the irregular shape contain?	9
2.	How many parts that are a half square or more does it contain?	8
3.	Add the two amounts to find the approximate number of squares the shape contains.	17
4.	If each square on the shaded shape has an area of one square centimeter, what is its area?	$14\frac{1}{2}$ cm^2
5.	Which two numbers have a product of seven and a sum of eight?	1 and 7
6.	Write down the information, then work out the answer. A rectangular prism has a length of 7 cm, a width of 4 cm and a depth of 10 cm. Write its volume in cubic centimeters.	280 cm^3
7.	Is a ton of steel heavier than a ton of aluminum cans? _**Both weigh 1 ton.**_	No
8.	Which top view matches the isometric drawing?	B
9.	Rearrange the letters of "charm" to spell the name of a month.	March
ⓘ	Questions 10 to 14 are about the line graph on your sheet. It shows the profits made by a small business from 1990 to 2000.	
10.	What profit did the business make in 1991?	$20,000.00
11.	What profit did it make in 1993?	$25,000.00
12.	In which consecutive years did the business make the same profit?	1995 and 1996
13.	What was the most successful year shown on the graph?	1999
14.	In which year did the profit rise by $15,000.00 compared to the previous year?	1994
15.	Add the volumes on your sheet, then write the total on the answer line.	7.005 L
16.	Which match do you move to change capital "C" into capital "F"?	3
ⓘ	The last 4 questions are about the television viewing guide on your sheet. Times shown are in 24-hour time.	
17.	Using a.m. or p.m., write the time "Albert the Albatross" starts.	3:30 a.m.
18.	Using a.m. or p.m., write the time "Wheel of Doom" starts.	5:30 p.m.
19.	Which program is on at 1:30 a.m.?	basketball
20.	How long is the movie "Moon Men"?	$2\frac{1}{2}$ hrs

Activity Answers

1. (a) 1,000   (b) 1,500   (c) 2,000   (d) 2,500   (e) 3,000   (f) 3,500   (g) 4,000   (h) 4,500

1. _____ 6. _____ 11. _____ 16. _____

2. _____ 7. _____ 12. _____ 17. _____

3. _____ 8. _____ 13. _____ 18. _____

4. _____ 9. _____ 14. _____ 19. _____

5. _____ 10. _____ 15. _____ 20. _____

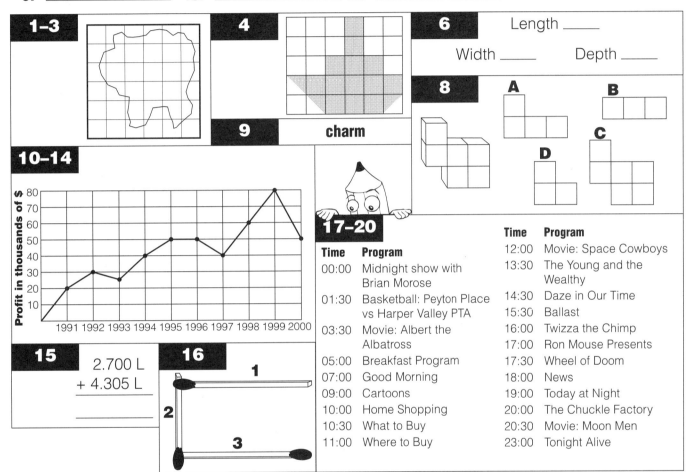

1–3

4

6 Length _____ Width _____ Depth _____

9 charm

8 A B C D

10–14

Profit in thousands of $

80 70 60 50 40 30 20 10

1991 1992 1993 1994 1995 1996 1997 1998 1999 2000

15
2.700 L
+ 4.305 L
_____

16
1
2
3

17–20

Time	Program
00:00	Midnight show with Brian Morose
01:30	Basketball: Peyton Place vs Harper Valley PTA
03:30	Movie: Albert the Albatross
05:00	Breakfast Program
07:00	Good Morning
09:00	Cartoons
10:00	Home Shopping
10:30	What to Buy
11:00	Where to Buy

Time	Program
12:00	Movie: Space Cowboys
13:30	The Young and the Wealthy
14:30	Daze in Our Time
15:30	Ballast
16:00	Twizza the Chimp
17:00	Ron Mouse Presents
17:30	Wheel of Doom
18:00	News
19:00	Today at Night
20:00	The Chuckle Factory
20:30	Movie: Moon Men
23:00	Tonight Alive

Activity   Multiplying by multiples of 50

Do the addition below. In each case you are adding 10 sets of the same number. Write answers in the answer spaces and then use this information to complete the number sentences.

A	B	C	D	E	F	G	H
20	30	40	50	60	70	80	90
20	30	40	50	60	70	80	90
20	30	40	50	60	70	80	90
20	30	40	50	60	70	80	90
20	30	40	50	60	70	80	90
20	30	40	50	60	70	80	90
20	30	40	50	60	70	80	90
20	30	40	50	60	70	80	90
20	30	40	50	60	70	80	90
+ 20	+ 30	+ 40	+ 50	+ 60	+ 70	+ 80	+ 90

Number sentences

(a) 50 x 20 = _____

(b) 50 x 30 = _____

(c) 50 x 40 = _____

(d) 50 x 50 = _____

(e) 50 x 60 = _____

(f) 50 x 70 = _____

(g) 50 x 80 = _____

(h) 50 x 90 = _____

BLAST 24

No.	Question and Discussion	Answer
1.	The square grid is made up of 100 squares. 75 are shaded. What fraction is shaded?	$^{75}/_{100}$
2.	What fraction is unshaded?	$^{25}/_{100}$
3.	Write the fraction shaded as a decimal.	0.75
4.	Write the fraction unshaded as a decimal.	0.25
5.	Write the fraction shaded as a percentage.	75%
6.	Write the fraction unshaded as a percentage.	25%
7.	At which of the times on your sheet do the hands of an analog clock form an acute angle?	8:55
8.	Which length shown for question 8 equals $2^1/_4$ meters?	2.25 m
9.	Look at the front, top and side views on your sheet. Which isometric drawing do they match?	A
10.	Draw a top view of Larry.	teacher
11.	How many are four 25s?	100
12.	How many are eight 25s?	200
13.	Add the measurements on your sheet and convert the answer to meters.	22 m
14.	Circle a number in the group that is a prime number.	5 or 7

(i) The last 6 questions are about the line graph on your sheet. It shows the number of minivans, cars and trucks sold by a dealership in a year. Notice the different kind of line used for each type of vehicle. Use abbreviations to answer when month names are needed.

No.	Question and Discussion	Answer
15.	How many trucks were sold in April?	18
16.	How many minivans were sold in January?	5
17.	In which month were the same number of cars and trucks sold?	August
18.	Which was the best month for the sale of minivans?	June
19.	How many minivans were sold altogether?	110
20.	How many vehicles were sold altogether in December?	21

Activity Answers

1. (a) 5   (b) 8   (c) 3 & 7   (d) 4   (e) 72   (f) 25   (g) 6

1. _____   6. _____   11. _____   16. _____
2. _____   7. _____   12. _____   17. _____
3. _____   8. _____   13. _____   18. _____
4. _____   9. _____   14. 4 5 6 7 8 9   19. _____
5. _____   10. _____   15. _____   20. _____

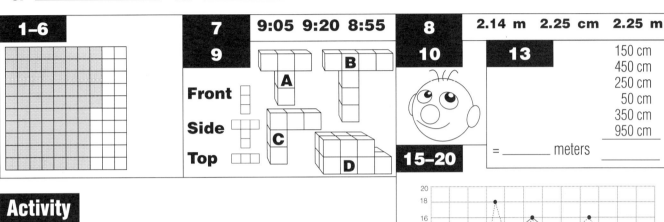

1–6

7 9:05 9:20 8:55

9 Front Side Top A B C D

8 2.14 m 2.25 cm 2.25 m

10

13
150 cm
450 cm
250 cm
50 cm
350 cm
950 cm

= _____ meters

15–20

Activity

Bar Graph

Batting Results

1. The bar graph shows the runs scored by a baseball team during a twelve-day road trip.

(a) How many runs were scored on the first day?

_____

(b) On what day/days were the most runs scored?

_____

(c) On what day/days were the least runs scored?

_____

(d) What was the most common number of

runs scored per day? _____

(e) What was the total number of runs scored?

_____

(f) How many runs were scored in total on

days 4, 7, 9 and 12? _____

(g) What was the average runs scored per day

on the trip? _____

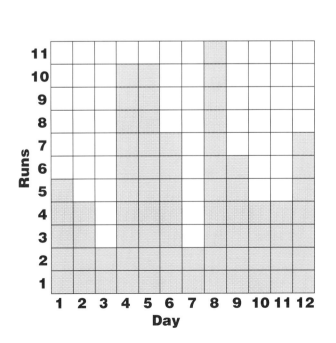

VEHICLES

Jan Feb Mar Apr May Jun Jul Aug Sept Oct Nov Dec

Minivans _____   Cars _ _ _   Trucks ....

Runs

1 2 3 4 5 6 7 8 9 10 11 12

Day

No.	Question and Discussion	Answer
1.	Which two numbers together have a sum of 10 and a product of 16?	2 and 8
2.	Divide 64 by 3. Write your answer on the answer line. Is there a remainder?	21, yes 1

For a number to be evenly divisible by three, its digits must add to 3, 6, or 9. The digits in 64 add to 10 which then (1 + 0) adds to one.

No.	Question and Discussion	Answer
3.	At which of the times on your sheet do the hands of an analog clock make a straight angle?	8:10
4.	Which amount listed for question 4 equals 750 milliliters?	$^3/_4$ L
5.	Which picture shows a cross section of a tennis ball?	A

(i) Questions 6 to 10 are about the weather chart on your sheet. The weather chart is a type of graph. Study the key. The pictures tell what the weather was like on a particular day.

No.	Question and Discussion	Answer
6.	On how many days were strong winds recorded?	2
7.	What sort of weather followed immediately after the windy days?	sunny
8.	How many days had rain?	11
9.	If baseball games are on Fridays, how many times do you think they may have been canceled in that month?	2
10.	What was the weather like on the last Tuesday of the month?	rainy

(i) Choose the unit you would use to measure the area of each of the following. Use the abbreviations.

No.	Question and Discussion	Answer
11.	Which would you use to measure the area of the United States?	km^2
12.	Which would you use to measure the area of a wheat farm?	ha
13.	Which would you use to measure the area of flea's bedspread?	mm^2
14.	Which would you use to measure the area of carpet in a room?	m^2
15.	Which would you use to measure the area of $50.00 bill?	cm^2
16.	What is the volume of a rectangular prism with the measurements given?	$350\ cm^3$
17.	Add the volumes on your sheet. Write the total on answer line 17.	8.31 L or 8.310 L

(i) The last 3 questions are about 5Z's classroom.

No.	Question and Discussion	Answer
18.	What is the area of the classroom?	$25\ m^2$
19.	What is the area of the storeroom?	$10\ m^2$
20.	What is the combined area of the storeroom and classroom?	$35\ m^2$

Activity Answers

1.
   (a) 5   (d) 6th
   (b) 5   (e) 53
   (c) 4th   (f) 51

1. _____ 6. _____ 11. _____ 16. _____
2. _____ 7. _____ 12. _____ 17. _____
3. _____ 8. _____ 13. _____ 18. _____
4. _____ 9. _____ 14. _____ 19. _____
5. _____ 10. _____ 15. _____ 20. _____

2 $3\overline{)64}$

3 7:15 8:10 8:30

4 $^3/_4$ mL $^3/_4$ L 7.5 L

5
A
B
C
D

6–10

sunny
overcast
thunderstorms
rainy
windy

April

Sun	Mon	Tues	Wed	Thurs	Fri	Sat
	1	2	3	4	5	6
7	8	9	10	11	12	13
14	15	16	17	18	19	20
21	22	23	24	25	26	27
28	29	30	31			

11–15

mm²
cm²
m²
ha
km²

16

Length = 10 cm
Width = 5 cm
Depth = 7 cm

17

$$\begin{array}{r} 4.875 \text{ L} \\ + 3.435 \text{ L} \\ \hline \end{array}$$

18–20

Store-room 2 m
Classroom 5 m
5 m

Activity *Line Graphs*

1. The line graph shows Scott and Karen's scores in a game of golf.

   The numbers along the bottom tell the hole being played. The numbers that go vertically tell the number of strokes taken to put the ball in the hole.

   Notice the different lines used to distinguish Scott's score from Karen's.

   (a) What was Scott's score on the first hole? _____

   (b) What did Karen score on the 5th hole? _____

   (c) On which hole did Scott and Karen score the same? _____

   (d) Which was Scott's best (lowest scoring) hole? _____

   (e) What was Scott's total score? _____

   (f) What was Karen's total score? _____

Hole 1st 2nd 3rd 4th 5th 6th 7th 8th 9th

Scott ——— **Karen** - - - - -

BLAST 26

No.	Question and Discussion	Answer
1.	Shapes that tessellate fit together without any spaces. Which shape on the sheet does not tessellate?	B
2.	All the things in Group A are Bluggs. None of the things in Group B are Bluggs. Which two things in Group C are Bluggs?	X and Y
	A Blugg must contain a circle.	
3.	Add the digits in 72. Will 3 divide into it without leaving a remainder?	yes
	Digits add to 9. For 3 to divide into a number without leaving a remainder, its digits must add to 3, 6, or 9.	
4.	Round 2,950 to the nearest 100.	3,000
5.	When we square a number we multiply it by itself. How many is 3 squared?	9
6.	What is the best (shortest, simplest) way of writing 4 kilometers 700 meters in decimal form?	4.7 km
7.	250 milliliters equals a quarter of a liter. What fraction of a liter is 750 mL?	$^3/_4$
8.	The square grid is made up of 100 squares. Seven are shaded. What fraction is shaded?	$^7/_{100}$
9.	What fraction is unshaded?	$^{93}/_{100}$
10.	Write the fraction shaded as a decimal.	0.07
11.	Write the fraction unshaded as a decimal.	0.93
12.	Write the fraction shaded as a percentage.	7%
13.	Write the fraction unshaded as a percentage.	93%
14.	Listen to the clues and try to work out the number I'm thinking of. Cross out the numbers that don't belong as we go. CLUE 1: It is an odd number. CLUE 2: It's a single digit number. CLUE 3: Three divides into it without leaving a remainder. CLUE 4: It's more than half a dozen. It is …	9
15.	Which shape's area can you find by multiplying the base by the height and then dividing by two?	triangle

(i) Choose from the words in the word bank to answer the last 5 questions.

No.	Question and Discussion	Answer
16.	On which would you weigh yourself?	bathroom scale
17.	Which tells the time using a big hand and a little hand?	analog clock
18.	Which measures temperature?	thermometer
19.	Which tells you how far you've been on a trip in the car?	odometer
20.	On which could you make a triangle using rubber bands?	geoboard

Activity Answers

1. A, hexagon
   B, heptagon
   C, nonagon
   D, quadrilateral
   E, pentagon
   F, octagon
   G, decagon

1. _____   6. _____   11. _____   16. _____

2. _____   7. _____   12. _____   17. _____

3. _____   8. _____   13. _____   18. _____

4. _____   9. _____   14. _____   19. _____

5. _____   10. _____   15. _____   20. _____

1
A B
C D

2 A | B | C
W X Y Z

4   2,950

6   4 km 700 m   4.7 km   4.70 km   4.700 km

8–13

14   1 2 3 4 5 6 7 8 9
10 11 12 13 14 15 16 17 18

15   square   circle   triangle   rectangle

16–20
(a) geoboard   (b) bathroom scale
(c) analog clock   (d) thermometer
(e) stethoscope   (f) odometer

Activity   *Regular and irregular shapes*

1. Most of the shapes you learn about will be regular. This means that the sides are the same length. All regular polygons have irregular equivalents. Use different colored lines to match the regular polygons with their irregular partners.

Regular

quadrilateral   pentagon   hexagon   heptagon   octagon   nonagon   decagon

Irregular

A   B   C   D   E   F   G

BLAST 27

No.	Question and Discussion	Answer
1.	Look at the diagram showing a patio and barbecue area. What is the area of the patio?	24 m^2
2.	What is the area of the barbecue?	6 m^2
3.	What is the combined area of the two?	30 m^2
4.	All of the things in Group A are Splurgs. None of the things in Group B are Splurgs. Which two things in Group C are Splurgs?	S and T

Splurgs have an even number of hairs on their heads.

(i) The next 4 questions are about the cakes on your sheet.

5.	As you can see, there are two whole cakes with frosting. Both have been cut up into 100 equal-sized pieces. Hungry Hank has nibbled away some of the frosting on the second cake. Write a mixed numeral (whole number and fraction) to tell how many frosted slices there are.	$1^{65}/_{100}$
6.	What fraction of a cake has no frosting?	$^{35}/_{100}$
7.	Write the amount with frosting as a decimal.	1.65
8.	Write the amount without frosting as a decimal.	0.35
9.	Which is the correct shadow for the flagpole?	F
10.	Amanda has a doctor's appointment at a quarter to four in the afternoon. The car breaks down so she arrives 23 minutes late. Write her arrival time in 24-hour time.	16:08
11.	Circle the number on the answer line that is not a factor of 36.	16
12.	Which two shapes can be put together to make a tessellating pattern?	B and D
13.	Which of the lengths listed is the simplest (best, shortest) way of writing 8 kilometers 200 meters?	8.2 km
14.	If each square on the shaded shape has an area of 1 square centimeter, what is the area of the shape?	18 cm^2
15.	Listen to the clues to find the mystery number.	
	CLUE 1: It's more than 200.	
	CLUE 2: It's an even number.	
	CLUE 3: Ten doesn't divide into it evenly.	
	CLUE 4: If you add the digits together they total 8. It's also the number of bones in the human body.	206
16.	How many legs do four sheep and three ducks have altogether?	22

(i) Look at the code on your sheet. Use it to answer the last 4 questions. Write your final answer on the answer lines.

17.		1 + 5 + 4 = 10
18.		3 + (2 x 7) = 17
19.		8 + (9 − 6) = 11
20.		6 x 5 = 30

Activity Answers

1. (a) 6,B   (b) 4,C   (c) 3,C   (d) 1,C   (e) alligator

1. _____   6. _____   11. 2 4 6 9 16   16. _____
2. _____   7. _____   12. _____   17. _____
3. _____   8. _____   13. _____   18. _____
4. _____   9. _____   14. _____   19. _____
5. _____   10. _____   15. _____   20. _____

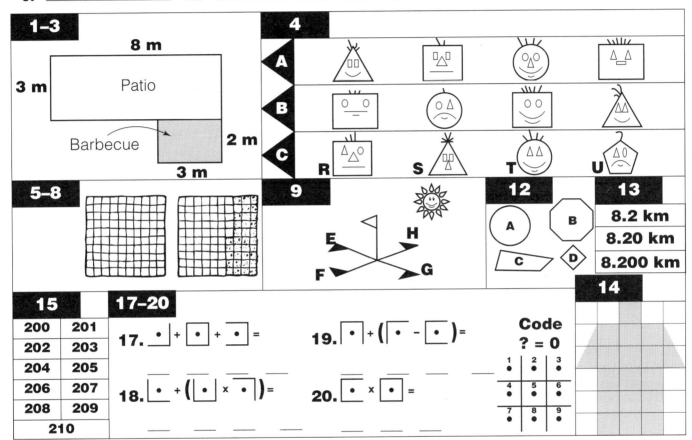

Activity

Grid Maps

1. When looking for a town or city in the index of most atlases, a grid reference is given. Refer to the grid map of the United States to answer the questions.

   (a) What is the grid position of the fish? _____

   (b) What is the grid position of the flower? _____

   (c) What is the position of the raven? _____

   (d) What is the apple's grid reference? _____

   (e) What is in position 5, D?

   It is an ___ ___ ___ ___ ___ ___ ___ ___.

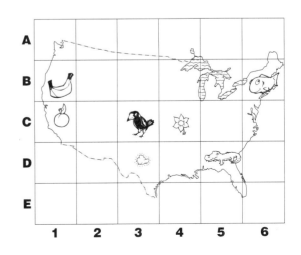

BLAST 28

No.	Question and Discussion	Answer
1.	Which is the correct shadow for the pyramid?	Y
2.	The picture shows a bathroom and laundry room. What is the area of the bathroom?	32 m²
3.	What is the area of the laundry room?	9 m²
4.	What is the combined area of both rooms?	41 m²
5.	Add the volumes on your sheet, then write the total on answer line 5.	8.310 L or 8.31 L
(i)	Questions 6 to 8 are about the thermometers on your sheet.	
6.	Which shows a healthy person's body temperature?	B
7.	Which shows the boiling point of water?	A
8.	Which shows the temperature of water from the hot water faucet?	C
9.	All the things in Group A are Globs. None of the things in Group B are Globs. Which two things in Group C are Globs?	W and X

Globs have an odd number of sides, a curved mouth and one wavy hair on their heads.

No.	Question and Discussion	Answer
10.	List the four prime numbers between 10 and 20.	11, 13, 17, 19
11.	Sydney Harbour Bridge was opened on Thursday, March 29, 1932. Write this using the short date form.	3/29/1932
12.	Dick and Dora Mouse ate some of the cheese on your sheet. Dick ate the striped pieces. Write the amount he ate as a decimal.	0.3
13.	Dora ate the bits with mold spots on them. Write the amount she ate as a decimal.	0.4
14.	Write the total amount eaten as a decimal.	0.7
15.	Which shape is a regular hexagon?	V
16.	Which shape is an irregular hexagon?	Z
17.	Which shape is an irregular heptagon?	Y
18.	Draw the shape that would appear on the shaded face of the die.	+
19.	What day was it four days before Tuesday?	Friday
20.	Thanksgiving is in the last month of fall. Which month is this? Write the abbreviation.	Nov.

Activity Answers

1. (a) fish
    (b) dogs
    (c) horses
    (d) cats

1. _____   6. _____   11. _____   16. _____

2. _____   7. _____   12. _____   17. _____

3. _____   8. _____   13. _____   18. _____

4. _____   9. _____   14. _____   19. _____

5. _____   10. _____   15. _____   20. _____

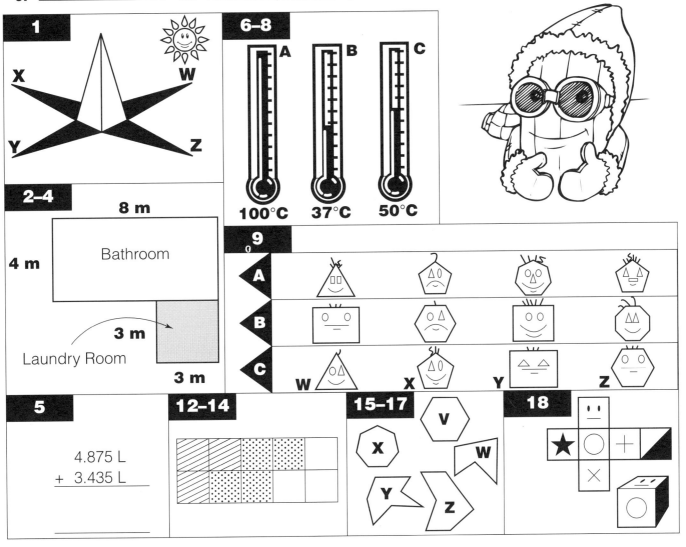

1

6–8
A   B   C
100°C   37°C   50°C

2–4
8 m
Bathroom
4 m
3 m
Laundry Room
3 m

9
A
B
C
W   X   Y   Z

5
4.875 L
+ 3.435 L
_____

12–14

15–17
V
X
W
Y
Z

18

Activity   *Pie Chart*

1. A pie chart can be used to show information. It can also be called a "sector graph." The children of Grade 5 were asked which pets they would most like to have. The results were recorded on the pie chart.

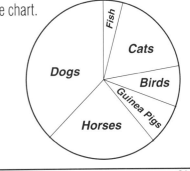

Fish
Cats
Dogs
Birds
Guinea Pigs
Horses

  (a) Which pet was written down by the smallest number of people?   _____

  (b) Which pet did nearly half the class prefer?   _____

  (c) Which was second most popular?   _____

  (d) Which were more popular, cats or birds?   _____

BLAST 29

No.	Question and Discussion	Answer
1.	Velma Mouse ate three whole cakes and $37/_{100}$ of a cake. Write the amount she ate as a mixed numeral.	$3^{37}/_{100}$
2.	Kevin Mouse ate four whole cakes and $12/_{100}$ of a cake. Write this amount as a mixed numeral.	$4^{12}/_{100}$
3.	How many whole cakes did they eat altogether?	7
4.	What was the combined amount of the fraction parts they ate?	$49/_{100}$
5.	How much cake did they eat altogether? Your answer should be a mixed numeral.	$7^{49}/_{100}$
6.	Look at the region ABCDEF. Side BC is 12 cm long. Side ED is 3 cm long. Can you work out how long side AF is?	9 cm; i.e., 12 cm – 3 cm
7.	Side AB is 10 cm long. Side DC is 7 cm long. Can you work out how long side EF is?	3 cm; i.e., 10 cm – 7 cm
8.	Draw lines to break the region into two rectangles, then find the total area by working out the areas of both rectangles and adding them together.	111 cm^2
9.	All the things in Group A are Grimes. None of the things in Group B are Grimes. Which 2 things in Group C are Grimes?	G and H

Grimes have a triangle and a curved line in them.

No.	Question and Discussion	Answer
10.	Draw the net of a square pyramid.	
11.	What is the best way of writing 7 kilometers 400 meters?	7.4 km
12.	Add 99 and 38 and write their total.	137
13.	The film "The Longest Story" lasts for three hours and 39 minutes. How many minutes is this altogether?	219 min
14.	If each square on the shaded shape has an area of one square centimeter, what is the area of the shape?	20 cm^2
15.	Justin is paid $9.00 an hour to mow the lawn. How much does he get if it takes him 1 $^1/_2$ hours?	$13.50

ⓘ Use the abbreviations for the name of the months to answer questions 16 to 18.

No.	Question and Discussion	Answer
16.	Mother's Day is in the last month of spring. Which month is this?	May
17.	Labor Day is in the first month of fall. Which month is this?	Sept.
18.	Independence Day is in the middle month of summer. Which month is this?	Jul.
19.	Write down Henry's scores in his last three math tests, then calculate his average. His scores were 6, 11 and 13.	10
20.	Which letter would appear on the shaded face of the die?	A

Activity Answers

Fraction	Decimal	Percentage
$35/_{100}$	0.35	35%
$75/_{100}$	**0.75**	**75%**
$33/_{100}$	**0.33**	**33%**
$99/_{100}$	**0.99**	**99%**
$7/_{10}$	0.7	70%
$3/_{10}$	**0.3**	**30%**
$1/_{10}$	0.1	**10%**
$9/_{10}$	**0.9**	90%

BLAST 29 WORKSHEET

A BLAST OF MATH

1. _____
2. _____
3. _____
4. _____
5. _____

6. _____
7. _____
8. _____
9. _____
10. _____

11. _____
12. _____
13. _____
14. _____
15. _____

16. _____
17. _____
18. _____
19. _____
20. _____

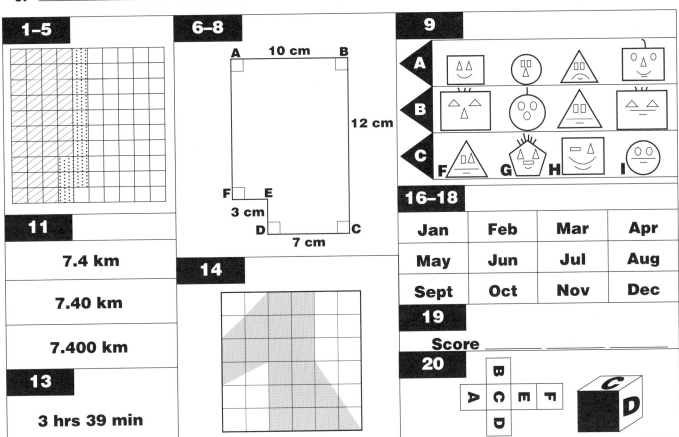

1–5

6–8

A ── 10 cm ── B

12 cm

F E
3 cm
D ──── C
7 cm

9

A
B
C
F   G   H   I

11

7.4 km

7.40 km

7.400 km

13

3 hrs 39 min

14

16–18

Jan	Feb	Mar	Apr
May	Jun	Jul	Aug
Sept	Oct	Nov	Dec

19

Score _____

20

B
A C E F
D

C
D

Activity

1. Complete the table.

	Fraction	Decimal	Percentage
(a)	$^{35}/_{100}$	0.35	35%
(b)	$^{75}/_{100}$		
(c)	$^{33}/_{100}$		
(d)	$^{99}/_{100}$		
(e)	$^{7}/_{10}$	0.7	70%
(f)	$^{3}/_{10}$		
(g)		0.1	
(h)			90%

Books Available from World Teachers Press®

MATH

A Blast of Math
> Grades 3-4, 4-5, 5-6, 6-7

Math Word Puzzles
> Grades 5-8

Mastergrids for Math
> Elementary Resource

Essential Facts and Tables
> Grades 3-10

Math Puzzles Galore
> Grades 4-8

Practice Math
> Grades 4, 5, 6, 7

Math Speed Tests
> Grades 1-3, 3-6

Problem Solving with Math
> Grades 2-3, 4-5, 6-8

Math Through Language
> Grades 1-2, 2-3, 3-4

Exploring Measurement
> Grades 2-3, 3-4, 5-6

Chance, Statistics & Graphs
> Grades 1-3, 3-5

Step Into Tables
> Elementary

Problem Solving Through Investigation
> Grades 5-8, 7-10

The Early Fraction Book
> Grades 3-4

The Fraction Book
> Grades 5-8

It's About Time
> Grades 2-3, 4-5

Do It Write Math
> Grades 2-3

Mental Math Workouts
> Grades 4-6, 5-7, 6-8, 7-9

Math Grid Games
> Grades 4-8

High Interest Mathematics
> Grades 5-8

Math Homework Assignments
> Grades 2, 3, 4, 5, 6, 7

Visual Discrimination
> Grades 1-12

Active Math

Math Enrichment
> Grades 4-7

Time Tables Challenge

30 Math Games
> PreK-1

Early Skills Series:
> Addition to Five, Counting and
> Recognition to Five, Cutting Activities,
> Early Visual Skills

Spatial Relations
> Grades 1-2, 3-4, 5-6

High Interest Geometry
> Grades 5-8

Money Matters
> Grades 1, 2, 3

LANGUAGE ARTS

Multiple-Choice Comprehension
> Grades 2-3, 4-5, 6-7

My Desktop Dictionary
> Grades 2-5

Spelling Essentials
> Grades 3-10

Reading for Detail
> Grades 4-5, 6-7

Writing Frameworks
> Grades 2-3, 4-5, 6-7

Spelling Success
> Grades 1, 2, 3, 4, 5, 6, 7

My Junior Spelling Journal
> Grades 1-2

My Spelling Journal
> Grades 3-6

Cloze Encounters
> Grades 1-2, 3-4, 5-6

Comprehension Lifters
> 1, 2, 3, 4

Grammar Skills
> Grades 2-3, 4-5, 6-8

Vocabulary Development   through
Dictionary Skills
> Grades 3-4, 5-6, 7-8

Recipes for Readers
> Grades 3-6

Step Up To Comprehension
> Grades 2-3, 4-5, 6-8

Cloze
> Grades 2-3, 4-5, 6-8

Cloze in on Language
> Grades 3-5, 4-6, 5-7, 6-8

Initial Sounds Fold-Ups

Phonic Sound Cards

Early Activity Phonics

Activity Phonics

Early Phonics in Context

Phonics in Context

Build-A-Reader

Communicating
> Grades 5-6

Oral Language
> Grades 2-3, 4-5, 6-8

Listen! Hear!
> Grades 1-2, 3-4, 5-6

Phonic Fold-Ups

Word Study
> Grades 2-3, 4-5, 6-7, 7-8

Draw to a Cloze
> Grades 5-8

Classical Literature
> Grades 3-4, 5-6, 5-8

High Interest Vocabulary
> Grades 5-8

Literacy Lifters
> 1, 2, 3 ,4

Look! Listen! Think!
> Grades 2-3, 4-5, 6-7

Teach Editing
> Grades 2-3, 3-4, 5-6

Proofreading and Editing
> Grades 3-4, 4-8, 7-8

High Interest Language
> Grades 5-8

Comprehend It!
> Grades 1-3, 4-5, 6-8

Comprehension for Young Readers

Language Skill Boosters
> Grades 1, 2, 3, 4, 5, 6, 7

Phonic Charts

Vocabulary Sleuths
> Grades 5-7, 6-9

Early Theme Series:
> Bears, Creepy Crawlies, The Sea

Phonics in Action Series:
> Initial Sounds, Final Consonant
> Sounds, Initial Blends and
> Digraphs, Phonic Pictures

OTHERS

Exploring Change
> Grades 3-4, 5-6, 7-8

Ancient Egypt, Ancient Rome,
Ancient Greece
> Grades 4-7

Australian Aboriginal Culture
> Grades 3-4, 5-6, 7-8

Reading Maps
> Grades 2-3, 4-5, 6-8

The Music Book
> Grades 4-8

Mapping Skills
> Grades 2-3, 3-4, 5-6

Introducing The Internet

Internet Theme Series:
> Sea, The Solar System,
> Endangered Species

Art Media

Visit us at:
www.worldteacherspress.com
for further information and free
sample pages.